GUIDE TO COMMON GRASSES

of the

Luangwa Valley, Zambia

Written and illustrated by

Pam Guhrs-Carr

Contributing Author/Editor

Richard Jeffery, MSc

Gadsden Publishers
P.O. Box 32581, Lusaka, Zambia

Elephant photograph on cover: Paula French. Shutterstock
Zebra photograph on inside front cover: Edward Selfe

Proceeds from the sale of this book will be donated to the Wildlife and Environmental Conservation Society of Zambia

ISBN 978-9982-24-160-1

About the Wildlife & Environmental Conservation Society of Zambia

Protecting Nature is our responsibility. Founded in 1953, the Wildlife & Environmental Conservation Society of Zambia (WECZ) is a charitable, membership- based NGO dedicated to promoting environmental conservation issues to all levels of the community. We organize Zambia's only nation-wide environmental education programs, spearhead community-based conservation efforts in key ecosystems, and advocate for conservation policies. Our work is built around four focus areas

1. **Forests & Wildlife Conservation**. We protect and restore Zambia's forests through community-led reforestation, alternative livelihoods and policy advocacy.
2. **Waste Management**. Plastic pollution is threatening the water, safety and health of Zambians. We are engaging Zambian communities to turn the tide through education and creating alternatives.
3. **Water & Climate Resilience**. We train and support thousands of our youth to lead the response to growing threats of climate change in Zambia.
4. **Policy Advocacy & Education**. Since independence WECSZ has played a leading role in lobbying and consulting. the government to create sustainable environmental policies, ranging from the creation of National Parks to the Water Bill and national climate adaptation plans.

About the Authors

Pam Guhrs-Carr grew up in Zambian wild places, with her conservationist father Norman Carr imparting in her from an early age a deep understanding of the bush. Pam's long career as a painter and observer of the environment has led naturally to her closely studying the wilderness, including grasses, of the Luangwa Valley which she calls home. She has written a tree book and a book on birds of prey. As a renowned wildlife artist, her work sells locally and internationally. She lives in Mfuwe with her dog Zanzi, where she creates art and runs art workshops with children.

Richard Jeffery, born in Uganda, has lived and worked in Africa most of his life, Zambia for the past 45 years. Richard is an applied ecologist, conservation biologist, wildlife business planner, and commercial pilot. He has worked with many local and international conservation NGOs and Government organisations, and published over 50 scientific papers and reports in his field, including co-author of *Kobus leche* in Jonathan Kingdon's Mammals of Africa Vol VI, and the WECSZ's Guides to "The Luangwa Valley National Parks", "Common Wild Mammals of Zambia", and "Reptiles, Amphibians & Fishes of Zambia".

CONTENTS

1 | Preface

Most botanical checklists available covering Zambia and the Luangwa in particular either require specialist technical knowledge, or are simply abbreviated lists tacked onto the end of other Guides or scientific reports.

This Guide is my contribution to publish something in between. As an amateur myself I have sought to keep the text as simple as practical but clear for the layman in illustrating and describing some of the more common grasses found around the riverine areas and foothills of the mid-Luangwa River valley of Zambia.

My intention is that it will provide a convenient basic reference for professionals and amateurs alike, while stimulating curiosity and interest in the latter to appreciate a most fascinating and important aspect of the habitat, ecology and diversity of wildlife in the Luangwa Valley ecosystem.

Because some of the grasses are notoriously difficult to identify, I am aware that I may not have achieved complete accuracy in this task, and that the Guide will have errors and omissions. In spite of the kind help I have received from many people, any mistakes are wholly my own, and I welcome comments, additions and corrections for possible *Addenda* to this edition and future revisions.

Pam Guhrs-Carr

2 | Introduction

I originally started work on this Guide in the early 1980s at a time when there were few guidebooks available for any of the grasses of southern Africa, and none for Zambia. Yet it was clear that there was a need for some sort of guide to the grasses of the Luangwa Valley, both for its growing tourism industry professionals and visiting scientists, as well as tourists and the general public.

By 1986, most of the work had been completed, but in the absence of funding to publish the Guide at that time, I printed a limited number of copies for use within our community of the "valley". The years flew by when Richard Jeffery, another valley hand and veteran wildlife ecologist, contacted me in early 2020 to suggest I could complete the job, with some minor additions, in order to provide what he thought would be, as originally intended, a layman's easy-to-use but valuable Guide as an introduction to grasses of the mid-Luangwa Valley, principally encompassing the South Luangwa National Park and surrounding Game Management Areas.

I personally feel this Guide will complement the growing number of superb but somewhat intimidating books for the more casual observer, and so with Richard's ecological and editorial assistance we have done just that, adding some interesting anecdotal perspectives of those individual "unsung heroes" so often over-looked like the grasses themselves, while keeping as much of the historical text as possible.

Grasses are of course important, but far more so than immediately meets the eye. Mike Bingham, regarding wild herbivores and their grazing impacts in the valley, pointed out that while less palatable grasses will not be as heavily grazed as more palatable grasses, moderate grazing is in fact essential for stimulating the growth and survival of all biotic grasslands.

Apart from their ecological significance, many "wild" grasses mentioned in this Guide are economically important among traditional communities, not least in the Luangwa Valley.

Grasses such as *Echinochloa colona* and *Oryza* spp. provide wild rice seed grain, while species such as *Setaria incrassata* (Kasense) and *Hyparrhenia* spp. are used extensively for thatching traditional dwellings. The common reed (*Phragmites mauritianus*) is used to make mattings, awnings, garden fencing and other light constructions, while bamboo (*Oxytenanthera abyssinica*) is used to make furniture and in building construction.

Another important grass of both ecological and economic significance in the valley (though not widespread) is the African vetiver (*Chrysopogon nigritanus [Vetiveria nigritana]),* often planted to prevent erosion and rehabilitate degraded grassland habitats.

We have included the original "Introduction to Grasses" for the Guide, written by James Milanzi (ZAWA/DNPW Ecologist, more lately with the African Parks Network), and the Guide's original synopsis of the Luangwa Valley's Grassland Ecology by Dr. Paul Smith, based on his work here in the 1990s in conjunction with "Bill" W.L. Astle and Dr Patrick Phiri.

Paul has continued to assist us, and we have followed his descriptions of grassland habitat types that feature most of the grasses depicted here, because it often helps identification by a process of elimination to be able to see in what kind of habitat a particular species of grass is likely to occur or not.

For the Kunda names we have used the "Dictionary of vernacular-scientific names of plants of the mid-Luangwa valley, Zambia" by W.L. Astle, P.S.M. Phiri and S.D. Prince (1997).

In presentation, this Guide largely follows the methodology of the "Guide to Grasses of Southern Africa" by Oudtshoorn (1999) favouring ease of field identification over taxonomy, and categorizing similar-looking species together as far as reasonably possible.

The Natural Resources Board of Zimbabwe "Common Veld Grasses of Rhodesia" by C. Lightfoot (1970) has proved helpful for identifying and checking botanical features of some of the grasses included in this Guide.

For this edition, we have not included sedges which are usually recognizable (although not always) by their triangular stems.

3 | Acknowledgements

Many people have encouraged and assisted me with preparation of this Guide over the years, for which I am ever grateful.

Back in the 1970s, an herbarium was established at the then National Parks and Wildlife Service (NPWS) Mfuwe HQ, under the auspices of Dr. William L. (Bill) Astle and Dr. Patrick S.M. Phiri. This guide would not have been possible without the original background of extensive research from these two remarkable botanists working in the Luangwa Valley.

A number of the pressed specimens and yellowed paper had stood in the shelves since then until its more recent upgrading. New cupboards and folders for specimens have energized the area and updated this fine little herbarium which has been invaluable for my work on this Guide.

I initially did the drawings for this Guide in the field over a succession of rainy seasons without knowing what most of them were. Mr. Dickson Sakala, a skilled local field amateur in the Mfuwe area, wrote up a list of some common species of grasses to guide me. He wrote in longhand from his own extensive notes, as he did not have any reference books, but it was his original list that provided the basis of my further work on this Guide. Sadly, Dickson passed away before we could collaborate fully to combine the text and drawings. His broad field knowledge was well known, his enthusiasm vast, and I am deeply grateful for the assistance of this unsung hero of the valley.

Mr. Wisdom Kabumbwe then assisted me in matching the drawings to names of specimens when we worked together inside the upgraded herbarium at the Zambia Wildlife Authority (ZAWA) offices at Chinzombo, making many forays into the field to check the material. I am grateful for his patience and enthusiasm to get the species list into shape.

I am most grateful to Dr. Patrick Phiri, the botanical expert of the Luangwa area who welcomed me into the Department of Biology at the University of Zambia and generously took the time to look at my material for the Guide, making invaluable comments, and showing me around the herbarium at the University.

Dr. Phiri has always been an enthusiastic force in the botanical arena in Luangwa and Zambia at large. He has done valuable work in the botanical field, and published many academic papers, articles, and a book on the vascular plants of Zambia. He was the Zambian co-coordinator of SABONET, which is a publication from the Southern African Botanical Diversity Network, a programme aimed at linking professional botanists and others in related fields in the ten countries of southern Africa from South Africa to Angola and Mozambique.

Patrick frequented the Luangwa area whenever he could, and was always in contact with local biologists working here. His teaching and influence have produced many Zambian specialists and a number of his ex-pupils have top positions in the botanical arena today. Patrick sadly passed away a while ago.

I am also very grateful to Mike Bingham, another of Zambia's prominent botanists with a fearsome knowledge of Zambian plants including Luangwa grasses, and who kindly read my text and made invaluable suggestions. Sadly, Mike passed away on 4th January, 2019.

Since Richard Jeffery and I started working to complete this Guide in 2020, a number of people have more recently stepped up to encourage and support us to this end for which we are very grateful.

In particular, we'd like to acknowledge Nicola Carruthers of the Wildlife & Environmental Conservation Society of Zambia (WECSZ, Lusaka Branch), for their support in fund-raising for this Guide; Nicholas Wightman (Zambeziflora), a leading contemporary Zambian botanist, who did the final technical proof-read and edit of the draft; Paul Golson, who edited the pdf illustrations; and the Aylmer May Cemetery Restoration Trust and an anonymous donor who helped finance printing of the Guide.

4 | The Luangwa Valley National Parks

The Luangwa Game Reserve was first gazetted in 1904, then later (1935) divided and gazetted into the North and South Luangwa Game Reserves. Today's Luangwa Valley National Parks were gazetted in 1972, including the South Luangwa (9,050 km^2), North Luangwa (4,636 km^2), Lukusuzi (2,720 km^2) and Luambe (254 km^2) National Parks, and their surrounding Game Management Areas (GMAs).

The Luangwa Valley is well-known for its exceptional biodiversity and was once renowned for providing refuge for some of the highest population densities of wild African elephants and black rhinos found anywhere, perhaps even higher than they should have been due to compression from habitat destruction and poaching outside the National Parks.

While such a distinction was devastated by some 90% towards the end of the last millennium due to years of brutal poaching and international wildlife trafficking of Zambia's priceless national heritage, elephant numbers are now increasing steadily and black rhinos beginning to appear again in the Luangwa Valley's magnificent landscape.

Today the valley's National Parks are recognized as internationally significant Protected Areas for conserving global biodiversity and essential ecosystem services supporting humanity's well-being and livelihoods through sustainable limits of development and acceptable use (such as tourism).

A variety of traditional rural communities live around the National Parks comprising languages including Cewa to the east of the valley, Senga and Tumbuka to the north, Nsenga to the south, Bisa and Lala to the west, while communities speaking Kunda and Ambo are clustered to the east of the South Luangwa National Park.

Traditional livelihoods include subsistence agriculture and hunting outside the National Parks in surrounding Game Management and Open Areas. Local communities are well aware of the socio-economic and environmental values of wildlife and natural resources and their responsibility to protect and manage them wisely.

5 | Introduction to Grasses of Luangwa Valley and their Ecological Importance

by James Milanzi, MSc, ZAWA Ecologist (ZAWA *now DNPW*)

Grasses form an important part of the biotic component of the ecosystem. They perform the full functions of plants, after utilizing sunlight to produce food. Grasses are therefore the basic building block of the food-chain: they are the primary producers on which primary consumers (grazers) feed and in turn secondary consumers (carnivores) feed on.

They provide grazers with fodder throughout the year, and mixed feeders with high protein options in the rainy season, thereby giving forbs, shrubs and trees a chance to flourish and provide browse for mixed feeders and browsers (grazers and browsers) when grasses have dried out to a lower nutritional status in the dry season.

They provide cover protecting the ground and soil from the erosive forces of rainwater, wind, animal trampling and ultra-violet light, aiding soil-moisture retention, and carbon dioxide sequestration (removing CO_2 from the atmosphere, a contributor to global warming).

Certain grasses have been planted in areas with serious erosion to prevent, contain and, in highly eroded areas, rehabilitate degraded grassland habitats.

Grasses are among the first plants to shoot up at the beginning of the rainy season, providing almost instant forage for herbivores after a long dry season.

For those people practicing selective crop production in agricultural lands, grasses may pose a challenge as weeds, and various conservation agriculture practices (biological control avoiding chemicals wherever possible) have been developed to control them.

In the Luangwa Valley, in addition to cultivated edible grasses such as maize and rice etc., in times of drought, because of their efficiency and drought-resistance, especially those that have a shorter growing season than cultivated edible grasses, local communities have survived on wild species such as *Echinochloa colona* and *Oryza longistaminata*, for edible seed-grain and wild rice. Such practices are becoming increasingly important in strengthening climate-change resilience through conservation and management of the productivity of natural ecosystems.

Grasses thus provide a source of food and income to local people who also sell it for making mats, brooms and fences, and for thatching roofs and building traditional dwellings, safari camps and lodges.

As a result, the world over, seed banks and herbariums are set up to store plant materials. In Zambia there are four herbariums, with our South Luangwa Area Management Unit having one at its HQ, Mfuwe.

6 | The Luangwa Valley's Grassland Ecology, a Synopsis of Grassland Habitat Types

by Dr Paul Smith

While my work was conducted mostly in the Luangwa River and its tributaries of the North Luangwa National Park (NLNP), similar riverine systems occur in the South Luangwa National Park (SLNP) including the Luangwa River itself and its major tributaries the Katete, Kapamba, Mushilashi and Luwi rivers, and the Chifungwe Plains.

These systems may thus all be conveniently divided into the following grassland Types and Sub-Types:

Type 1. *Chloris – Dactyloctenium – Echinochloa* **Valley floor secondary grasslands.** This takes the form of short, annual grassland punctuated with occasional clumps of *Combretum obovatum* thicket. Found in degraded mopane woodland associated with older alluvial soils away from the meander belt of the Luangwa River. These flat, low-lying soils are seasonally waterlogged. The soils tend to be shallow, poorly-drained, light grey, compacted, neutral sandy clays or sandy loams.

Type 2. Valley riverine grasslands. These are associated with the larger rivers in the valley with extensive floodplains and attendant meander belts, drainage channels and oxbows with deep stratified soil textures ranging from well-drained sand bars to black cracking clay.

2a. *Cynodon – Eragrostis* **grasslands on sandy soils.** These are the inside curves of the rivers and streams where the most common of the taller grasses are *Andropogon gayanus, Cymbopogon caesius, Digitaria milanjiana, Hyparrhenia filipendula, Hyperthelia dissoluta* and *Setaria sphacelata*. The common medium-sized grasses include *Dactyloctenium giganteum, Eragrostis cilianensis, Heteropogon contortus* and *Sporobolus pyramidalis*. The common smaller grasses include the ubiquitous *Cynodon dactylon* which forms carpets on the alluvial sandy soils of old ox-bows known as *wafwas*. This word means "dead river" in the Kunda language and describes the many old river courses which have developed into lagoons and swales. The other short species at the lower herbaceous levels include *Chloris virgata, Dactyloctenium aegyptium, Eleusine indica, Eragrostis ciliaris,* and *Urochloa mosambicensis*.

2b. Wooded *Setaria – Hyparrhenia* **grasslands on clay soils.** These are described as brown and black clay soils that are associated with the larger rivers and support distinctive tall grasslands. *Hyparrhenia rufa* is an important species on the brown clay and forms a large part of elephants' diet. On the black 'cotton' clay *Setaria incrassata* (*Kasense*) is an important grass for both people and wild animals as it is heavily browsed by elephants and is also collected annually by local people for thatching dwellings. It grows in large uninterrupted stands, a good example of which may be seen on the right-hand side of the road just before the entrance of the National Park. This kind of grassland habitat on clay often grades into a type of savannah woodland, which includes such trees as *Kigelia africana*, *Acacia* spp. and *Combretum* spp.

2c. Aquatic/semi-aquatic grasses. The water grasses associated with the flooded and water-logged clay areas in ox-bow lagoons and dambos of the Luangwa Valley are *Oryza barthii, Setaria incrassata, Echinochloa colona, Leersia hexandra*, and *Sporobolus pyamidalis*.

Type 3. Dambo *Loudetia simplex – Hyparrhenia* **grasslands.** This type of grassland is associated with the upper escarpments where the rivers and streams do not have a well-developed meander belt like the larger rivers on the valley floor. During the rainy season the dambos and streams are characterized by the grasses *Loudetia simplex,* and

Setaria sphacelata and later on in April/May *Hyparrhenia* species are common. There are also some species that are water-associated and which are the same as those found in the valley proper. These are *Digitaria milanjiana, Echinochloa colona, Setaria sphacelata, Sporobolus pyamidalis* and *Urochloa mosambicensis*.

However, much more extensive in both SLNP and NLNP is *Combretum-Terminalia-Diospyros* **wooded grassland**. This is a different kind of "sourveld" where the dominant grass is *Loudetia flavida* on the shallow, stony soils of the Muchinga foothills. The grass layer is well developed and dominated by medium to tall coarse grasses including *Andropogon fastigiatus, A. gayanus, A. schirensis, Aristida scabrivalvis, Diheteropogon amplectens, Heteropogon contortus, Hyparrhenia anemopaegma*, Loudetia flavida, Monocymbium ceresiiforme, Sorghum versicolor, Zonotriche inamoena* and *Bothriochloa bladhii,* mostly in poorly drained areas.

* *the only known endemic grass of the Luangwa Valley*

7 | Arrangement of this Guide

The following simple line drawings are intended to illustrate principal features of the grasses that will assist identification in the field.

For scaling, descriptions approximate sizes as small or short (< 500mm), medium (500-1,500mm), tall (1,500-2,500mm), and very tall (>2,500mm).

Illustrations are accompanied by descriptions of each grass for recognition in a general visual sense from their predominant features in order to assist with identification. Salient botanical features or habits are described, including some pointers regarding the ecology of the grasses such as the habitats in which they are likely to occur. The nutritional values and other values of the grasses to wildlife and local communities are briefly described.

Where possible we have described interesting or anecdotal features including locations of noteworthy stands and other features of specific grasses in and around the South Luangwa National Park.

Because this is by no means an exhaustive checklist of grasses of the Luangwa valley ecosystem, we have focused on the more commonly found or noteworthy species which one is most likely to encounter on a game drive or walk in the valley floor floodplains of the South Luangwa National Park and surrounding Game Management Areas.

Although our aim is to keep this Guide as technically simple as possible, we have preferred using Latin names as the principal references rather than common English ones which tend to be inconsistent.

However, we have included some English names where they conveniently describe obvious characteristics, such as the aromatic Turpentine grass, or the shape of the Herringbone grass. We have also included local Kunda names wherever possible, but these are also variable because one species of grass may have different Kunda names depending on locality.

While we have limited the use of botanical terms, some are particularly useful in combination with the illustrations for distinguishing between and identifying similar species; such terms are described briefly below.

Botanical terms

Grasses may be either **annual**, which means that they come to maturity in one year, or **perennial**, which means they take two or more years to complete their cycle.

Stolons are propagative runners, which grow horizontally above the ground while **rhizomes** are below the ground rooting from their joints.

Tufted means it grows low on the ground with many stems springing from the same spot. A **culm** is a stem out of which the leaves grow at the joints or **nodes.**

The **leaf sheath** is the part wrapped around the base of the leaf and stem while the **leaf blade** stands out independently from the stem.

The flower head or **inflorescence** bears the flowers and later the seeds. The actual flower of the grass has tiny petals, sometimes surprisingly bright, such as the yellow of *Hyparrhenia* spp. and the orange petals of *Oryza longistaminata.* These petals appear between two **bracts**, which are little modified leaves. Sometimes a bristle-like extension protrudes from a floret which is an **awn**, for example in *Heteropogon* and *Hyparrhenia.* If the inflorescence branch is subdivided into spikelets it is known as a **panicle.** If there are no subdivisions in the flowering head it is a **raceme** or a **spike.**

The following points are helpful to avoid confusion when identifying similar-looking grasses.

1. Look at the **inflorescence** because this is the least variable aspect within one species
2. If confronted with confusing species always compare the **awn**, a little hair in the **spikelet**, as this is usually diagnostic
3. Also look at the **node,** which is the thickened part on the stem like a joint in a limb; sometimes these are hairy and may be coloured red or purple, often diagnostic for certain species
4. It is useful to remember there are always variations in colour and shape depending on the maturity of the inflorescence; that of *Panicium maximum* and *Echinochloa colona* (*lupunga)* is bright red, almost purple, when ripe, but is whitish green when unripe; in the field *Oryza,* the rice grass, can look red or white depending on which stage it is in its growth cycle
5. There is a great variety in the **size** of grasses depending on fertility of the soil; because size is not always diagnostic, look carefully at the **spikelets** for identification
6. Not only are sizes and colour variable but also shape of the inflorescence; *Aristida congesta* for instance changes shape dramatically as it matures; others such as *Chloris virgata* change shape when dry or ripe
7. Look at the **leaf sheaths** and **leaf blades** to see if they are hairy (**hispid**) or not (**glabrous**), or if the margins are smooth, serrated, undulate or thickened
8. Look at the **ligule** against the culm where the leaf sheath and leaf blade are joined; it may be a membrane, a membrane with a hairy margin, or a ring of hairs

For clarity and simplicity in identification we have arranged and numbered the illustrations alphabetically in the species' list below according to their ***scientific*** names, followed by their local (*Kunda*) and English names where available, grouped according to four types of **inflorescences**, namely Paniculate, Solitary (unbranched), False Panicle, and Digitate, as described by Oudtshoorn (1999).

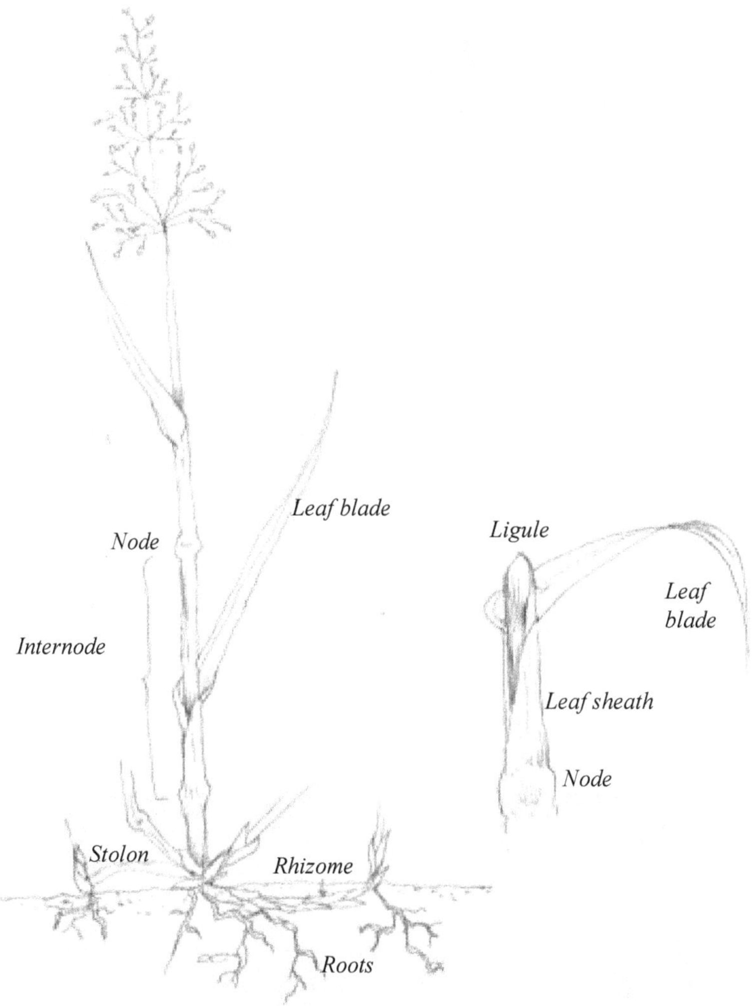

Typical Structure of a Grass

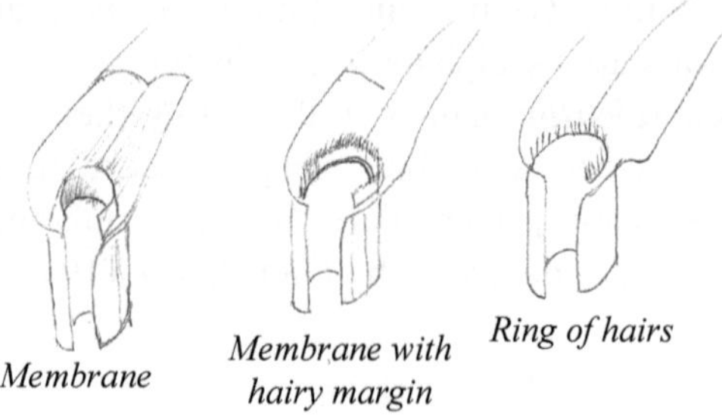

Types of Grass Ligules

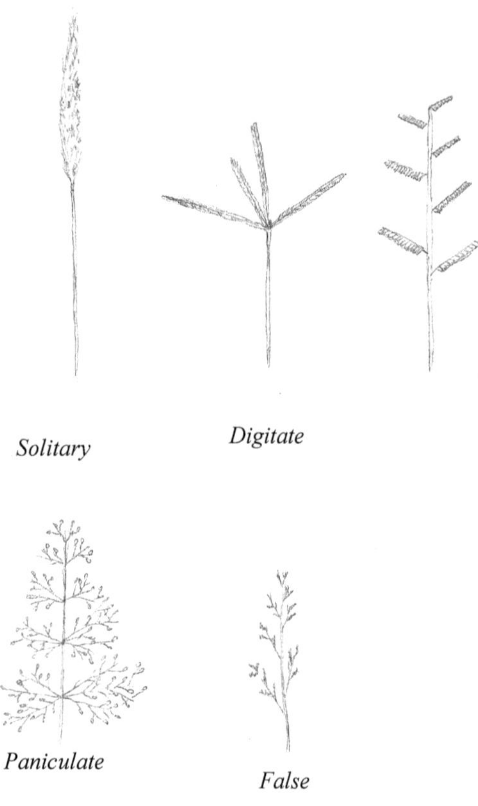

Types of Grass Inflorescences

PANICULATE (branched primary and secondary Axes)

1 Aristida congesta (Kasindainyu)

2 Aristida junciformis

3 Aristida rhiniochloa (Kasindainyu)

4 Eragrostis aethiopica

5 Eragrostis aspera (Kavundula)

6 Eragrostis cilianensis (Seshe)

7 Eragrostis ciliaris

8 Eragrostis gangetica (Bungamanene)

9 Eragrostis trichophora

10 Eragrostis viscosa

11 Imperata cylindrica

12 Leersia hexandra

13 Loudetia simplex (Luewo, Sempya, Sempia)

14 Melinis repens (Kankululu)

15 Oryza longistaminata (Mupunga, Ntukwe)

16 Oryza barthii (Chiole, Chuole)

17 Panicum coloratum (Gugu)

18 Panicum maximum (Mapuya, Nkwinde)

19 Panicum repens

20 Phragmites australis (Katete, Matete)

21 Sorghum versicolor **(***Mulu, Kaemena, Kandodo)*

22 Sporobolus festivus

23 Sporobolus panicoides

24 Sporobolus pyramidalis (Kalume kasepia)

25 Tristachya superba (Mpolwe)

SOLITARY (Spikes/Racemes rounded, flat, or one-sided)

26 Cenchrus ciliaris

27 Ctenium concinnum

28 Heteropogon contortus

29 Rottboellia cochinchinensis Synonym *exaltata (Zuya)* Itch grass

30 Setaria incrassata (Kasense)

31 Setaria pallide-fusca (Mpukusa)

32 Setaria sphacelata

FALSE PANICLE (branched primary Axis in groups of Racemes)

33 Andropogon eucomus

34 Cymbopogon excavatus (Museye) Synonym *A. caesius* Turpentine grass

35 Hemarthria altissima

36 Hyparrhenia filipendula (Hyparrhenia spp., Kavimbamkutu, Lupala, Numbu, Nkoche)

37 Hyparrhenia hirta

38 Hyparrhenia rufa

39 Hyperthelia dissoluta

40 Andropogon gayanus (Nyamalokoto)

DIGITATE (single/multiple Racemes/Spikes around primary Axis)

41 Bothriochloa insculpta

42 Chloris virgata (Nkombwa)

43 Chloris gayana

44 Cynodon dactylon (Kapinga)

45 Dactyloctenium aegyptium (Kambusa, Chimbusa)

46 Dactyloctenium giganteum

47 Digitaria diagonalis

48 Digitaria milanjiana (Lwiwa, Rwiwa)

49 Echinochloa colona (Lupunga, Chipunga, Malyamvuwu, Chikwanje)

50 Eleusine indica (Bule, Dulu)

51 Eriochloa stapfiana

52 Oplismenus hirtellus

53 Pogonarthria squarrosa (Kasense)

54 Setaria homonyma

55 Trichoneura grandiglumis

56 Urochloa mosambicensis (Nagapanda) Synonym *U. pullulans*

Finally, we have included a section of the Guide entitled "Field Notes" with a number of blank pages, for if this Guide is to fulfil its intended purpose it will be a convenient field companion in which users can record their own observations.

8 | Species' Descriptions and illustrations

This section presents systematic species' descriptions and my original pen and ink sketches. As such, some of the colourful beauty and charismatic features of grasses may be overlooked - the tall emergent bright green stems and leaves and yellow-orange florets turning into white inflorescences of *Oryza longistaminata*, remaining partly submerged for much of the rainy season, often accompanied by belly-deep grazing elephants (*Cover picture*) – the burnished silvery spikes of sunlit thatching grasses, through which a dazzle of zebra peers inquisitively (*inside Front Cover*).

PANICULATE INFLORESCENCES

***1 Aristida congesta* Roem. & Schult.** (*Kasindainyu)*
Tassel three awn

Description: Short-medium, tufted, culms erect, slender; inflorescence initially greenish, becoming white as it matures due to the long awns intertwining horizontally causing a fuzzy congested appearance on one or two densely compacted panicles; distinguished by single floret spikelets' twisted column and three long spiky awns (12 - 30 mm); leaves are glabrous and roll up when mature, long white hairs where the leaf blade meets the leaf sheath and culm, ligule inconspicuous

Habit: Weak perennial occasionally annual, flowering October to May
Ecology: Grows in most soil types but favours deep sandy clay or loamy soils; often on rocky ridges and stony hillsides, also in degraded habitats, settlements, cultivated lands, roadsides
Nutritional value: Low leaf production, limited grazing value
Other features: Resilient soil stabilizer in arid areas, indicator of habitat disturbance and over-grazing; similar to *A. c.* subsp. *barbicollis* which has an open panicle the seeds of which penetrate wildlife and livestock pelage causing irritation, damage and physical injury

***2 Aristida junciformis* Trin. & Rupr.**
Gongoni three awn

Description: Short-medium, densely tufted, culms slender, usually unbranched, ascending; inflorescence initially greenish, becoming whitish as it matures into a compacted panicle of spikelets with three long awns (15 - 20 mm); fine leaves, glabrous, usually rolled when mature, ligule inconspicuous
Habit: Weak perennial or annual, flowering November to May
Ecology: Grows in most soil types but favours gravelly soil on hillsides, loamy soils in open grasslands, and clay soils in dambos and wetland margins; also in degraded habitats, settlements, cultivated lands, roadsides

Nutritional value: Low leaf production of limited grazing value
Other features: Resilient soil stabilizer in arid areas, indicator of habitat disturbance and over-grazing; stems (culms) used for dense compacted "Barotse" thatching and to make hand-brooms

3 ***Aristida rhiniochloa Hochst.*** *(Kasindainyu)*
Rough three awn

Description: Short-medium, coarsely tufted, culms erect, branched, tinged purple; inflorescence a loosely contracted panicle maturing into a large flowering head, distinguished by single-floret purple brown hairless spikelets each with three long spiky awns (18 - 30 mm); upper leaf sheath has long white hairs
Habit: Annual, flowering January to May
Ecology: Commonly grows on gravelly soils or stony slopes, but also in degraded habitats, settlements, cultivated lands, roadsides
Nutritional value: Low leaf production, but useful grazing value in the absence of other grass cover
Other features: Resilient soil stabiliser in arid areas, indicator of habitat disturbance and over-grazing; a hardy grass, growing where most other grasses cannot survive

4 Eragrostis aethiopica Chiov.
Closely related to *Eragrostis tef* (Tef)

Description: Medium, tufted, erect or ascending culms, glabrous and without glands at the nodes; delicate open inflorescence, elliptic panicle, linear spikelets laterally compressed, 6 – 28 florets; leaves linear, flat or rolled, glabrous and without glands; leaf sheaths also glabrous; ligule a line of hairs
Habit: Annual, flowering November to May
Ecology: Floodplain grasslands, oxbow lagoons, and river banks; alluvial, sand or clay soils; also in degraded habitats, settlements, cultivated lands, roadsides
Nutritional value: Low leaf production, but useful grazing substitute, and seed may be used as grain in times of famine
Other features: Resilient soil stabilizer in arid areas, indicator of habitat disturbance and over-grazing

5 Eragrostis aspera (Jacq.) Nees (*Kavundula)* Rough love grass

Description: Small, tufted, multiple branching culms from base; inflorescence a large open spherical panicle, branches ascending expansively with bearded axils, and long, slender pedicles, giving the grass an airy, fluffy look; spikelets small and grouped together on short stalks, overlapping like fish scales, typical of *Eragrostis* spp.; inconspicuous open or folded leaves with prominent mid-rib and hispid ligules

Habit: Annual, flowering January to June

Ecology: Commonly grows in light shade, on sandy soils, often in degraded habitats, settlements, cultivated lands, roadsides **Nutritional value**: Little leaf production, limited grazing value **Other features**: Grows low to the ground with many stems springing from the same point, and its large inflorescence head sometimes detaches itself in the wind and rolls away on the ground; resilient soil stabiliser in arid areas, indicator of habitat disturbance and over- grazing

6 Eragrostis cilianensis (All.) Vignolo ex Janch *(Seshe)*
Stink love grass

Description: Short-medium, sparsely tufted, slanting culms branching and bending at the nodes; contracted panicle; unpleasant smell exuded by glandules on leaf margins and branches of inflorescence

Habit: Annual, flowering October to June

Ecology: Commonly grows on sandy soils, often around areas where rainwater collects, and degraded habitats, settlements, cultivated lands, roadsides

Nutritional value: Poor grazing value due to low leaf-production and unpalatability, nevertheless its seeds may be consumed by a variety of birds and insects, and anecdotally among drought- and famine-stricken communities

Other features: Potentially useful pioneer grass; indicator of habitat disturbance and over-grazing

7 Eragrostis ciliaris (L.) R.Br.
Woolly love grass

Description: Short-medium, tufted, culms, erect, slender; attractive woolly inflorescence, erect or drooping, contracted sometimes interrupted panicle, hispid spikelets densely clustered and usually flushed with red or purple; leaves bright green, open folded with rough margins
Habit: Annual, flowering all year
Ecology: Commonly grows on moist sandy soils, often in degraded habitats, settlements, cultivated lands, roadsides
Nutritional value: Low-average grazing value
Other features: Attractive inflorescence; indicator of habitat disturbance and over grazing

8 Eragrostis gangetica (Roxb.) Steud. (*Bungamanene)* Slimflower love grass

Description: Short-medium, loosely tufted, culms erect, decumbent or ascending, nodes glabrous; inflorescence an open (usually) branched panicle, spikelets laterally compressed, typical of *Erogrostis* spp.; leaves and leaf sheaths smooth; hairy ligules
Habit: Annual (or short-lived perennial), flowering January to May, sometimes all year
Ecology: Occurs on margins of dambos, floodplain grasslands, river banks, and in mopane and mixed deciduous woodlands on sandy loam soils; also in degraded habitats, settlements, cultivated lands, roadsides
Nutritional value: Average to good grazing value; used by local people as a food-grain and medicine; seeds consumed by a variety of birds and insects
Other features: Indicator of habitat disturbance and over-grazing

9 Eragrostis trichophora Coss. & Durieu
Hairy love grass

Description: Small, slender, tufted, culms wiry usually branched above the lower nodes, which are sometimes bent and rooting;

inflorescence is open panicle with purplish-yellow branches, whorled at the base with long hairs ("prickles") in the axils; spikelets typical of *Eragrostis* spp. (see *E. aspera* above); basal leaf sheaths hispid, papery, and the "nerves" are rounded and well apart at the base **Habit**: Perennial, flowering November to May

Ecology: Favours sandy, sandy loam or gravelly soils, where rainwater collects, often in degraded and eroded habitats, settlements, cultivated lands, roadsides

Nutritional value: Low grazing value

Other features: Useful soil stabilizer; indicator of habitat disturbance and over-grazing

10 Eragrostis viscosa (Retz.) Trin.

Sticky love grass

Description: Small, tufted, aromatic, the entire plant covered with tiny, viscid or sticky glands, culms branched often knee-like bent; inflorescence an open panicle, with small finely hispid spikelets, pink or reddish; leaves are finely tapered, initially straight, becoming progressively tangled as the plant matures

Habit: Annual, flowering January to August

Ecology: Typical of mopane woodland, and drier degraded habitats, settlements, cultivated lands, roadsides; indicator of shallow, compacted, unfertile sandy loam or clay soils

Nutritional value: Unpalatable, low leaf production and grazing value

Other features: Indicator of habitat disturbance and over-grazing

11 Imperata cylindrica (L.) Raeusch.

Silver spike, Cottonwool grass

Description: Short-medium, tufted, culms erect, unbranched; inflorescence a white, densely hispid contracted panicle; leaves coarse, hard, sharply tipped, with prominent mid-rib, turning reddish brown in the dry season; leaf sheaths round, smooth, becoming fibrous; ligule inconspicuous

Habit: Perennial creeping rhizomatous hydrophyte, flowering August to June

Ecology: Typically grows in wet, poorly drained alluvial soils in or around shallow permanent water, often in dense stands
Nutritional value: Poor grazing value, but rhizomes are nutritious
Other features: Extensive mat-like rhizomes may assist with flood-control in wet areas

12 Leersia hexandra Sw.
Rice grass

Description: Short-medium, tufted, culms erect, nodes ringed with short white hairs; inflorescence an open panicle, spikelets laterally compressed, hispid; coarse sharp leaves with prominent mid-rib
Habit: Perennial creeping rhizomatous hydrophyte, flowering all year
Ecology: Typically grows in water-logged alluvial soils in or around shallow permanent water, sometimes in dense stands
Nutritional value: Medium grazing value despite its coarse leaves, and its seeds may be consumed by a variety of birds and insects
Other features: Extensive mat-like rhizomes may assist with flood-control in wet areas; known for its ability to accumulate heavy metal contaminants from polluted soil and water

13 Loudetia simplex (Nees) C.E.Hubb. *(Luewo, Sempya, Sempia)*
Common russet grass

Description: Medium, tufted, culms erect, slender unbranched, nodes may be hispid; inflorescence loosely contracted panicle developing into large flowering head, spikelets with single, delicate long awn (25 - 50 mm); leaves sparse, lower leaf sheath often hispid
Habit: Perennial, flowering November to January, or all year **Ecology**: Grows on poor sandy soil in the open grassland and on hillsides, but also common in miombo woodland and edges of dambos **Nutritional value**: This grass is hard and unpalatable, low grazing value
Other features: Very similar to *L. flavida* which is more common on the valley floor, distinguished by glumes having sharp tips; indicator of infertile soil and over-grazing; fine culms bound and used for ("Barotse") thatching and sweeping brooms

14 Melinis repens (Willd.) Zizka subsp. *repens & subsp. grandiflora (Hochst.) Zizka (Kankululu)*
Natal red top

Description: Medium, tufted, culms ascending to erect, often rooting at lower nodes, hairy upper nodes; distinctive paniculate inflorescence, fluffy spikelets with silky white, pink to dark red or purple hairs, hispid; spikelets 2 - 4.5 mm long in subsp. *M. repens* and 5 - 12 mm long in subsp. grandiflora; leaves have prominent mid-rib, ligule an inconspicuous ring of hairs
Habit: Weak perennial, flowering September to June
Ecology: Subsp. *grandiflora* widespread in natural grassland habitats on all well-drained soil types, subsp. *repens* the more common pioneering grass in degraded habitats, settlements, cultivated lands, roadsides
Nutritional value: Low leaf production but palatable, providing average grazing value
Other features: Widespread pioneering grass; good soil stabilizing characteristics, indicator of habitat disturbance and over-grazing

15 Oryza longistaminata A.Chev. & Roehr. (*Mupunga, Ntuke)*
Wild, long stamen or red rice (cultivated rice is *O. sativa*)

Description: Tall, tufted, long creeping rhizomes, culms erect or ascending, sometimes floating, aerial rooting from nodes, bright green or whitish where submerged, smooth, glossy, usually glabrous, spongy; inflorescence long, dense, erect sometimes drooping panicle, stout angular rachis, numerous ascending racemes (branches), short hairs at base, spikelets pale green to brownish, awn pink-purple (40 - 75 mm); leaf sheaths pale green-brown, becoming flaky, leaves bright to dark green, ligule tall triangular membrane
Habit: Perennial, extensively branched, creeping, rhizomatous hydrophyte, flowering October to May; distinguished from *O. barthii* by its greater height and shorter awns
Ecology: Associated with waterlogged areas and may be seen in the same habitats as O. *barthii*, *Echinochloa colona, Leersia hexandra* and *Sporobolus pyramidalis;* favours clay or black cotton soils (vertisols)

Nutritional value: Palatable, high grazing value; rice-like seeds are eaten in times of famine, and are also consumed by a variety of birds and insects
Other features: This grass grows in abundance on the floodplain and swampy areas around Mfuwe and the game-viewing spurs in the SLNP

16 Oryza barthii A.Chev. (*Chiole, Chuole*)
Barth's, wild or African wild rice (cultivated African rice is *O. glaberrima*)

Description: Medium, weakly tufted, culms erect or bending and ascending, smooth, glossy, usually glabrous, spongy, rooting from lower nodes; inflorescence long, dense, erect sometimes drooping panicle, stout angular rachis, numerous ascending racemes (branches) some appressed to rachis, spikelets pale green to straw-coloured, long pink purple awns (80 - 160 mm); leaf sheaths pale green-brown, becoming flaky, long bright green leaves, short usually rounded membranous ligule
Habit: Annual, rhizomatous hydrophyte, flowering February to March
Ecology: Grows around patches of deep water in the seasonally flooded oxbows, floodplains and dambos of the Luangwa river, and water-logged areas of mopane or munga (savanna) woodland and similar open habitats; may be seen in the same habitats as *O. longistaminata*, *Echinochloa colona, Leersia hexandra* and *Sporobolus pyramidalis*; favours clay or black cotton soils (vertisols) **Nutritional value**: Palatable, high grazing value; rice-like seeds are eaten in times of famine, and are also consumed by a variety of birds and insects
Other features: Progenitor of cultivated *Oryza glaberrima*, African rice; less common in the valley than *O. longistaminata* and distinguished by significantly longer awns

17 Panicum coloratum L. (*Gugu*)
Small buffalo grass

Description: Medium-tall, tufted; inflorescence is an open panicle, spreading, one or two lower branches, small purplish spikelets, no awns or hairs; broad leaves and lower leaf sheaths rough and densely hispid; ligule ring of small white hairs

Habit: Perennial, short rhizomes, flowering October to May **Ecology**: Grows on a variety of soils from sandy loam to clay, next to streams or in their drainage courses and depressions
Nutritional value: Palatable and high grazing value persisting well into the dry season; its seed-grain is consumed by a variety of birds and insects, and by local communities in times of famine
Other features: Drought resistant

18 Panicum maximum Jacq. (*Mapuya, Nkwinde)*
Guinea or Buffalo grass

Description: Very tall, tufted, leafy; central upright culms from which long thin side branches grow, often spreading before growing vertically; inflorescence a large open panicle, loosely branched, lower ones whorled, small purplish spikelets, no awns or hairs; leaves very broad (broader than *P. coloratum*), leaves and leaf sheaths around the stem hispid
Habit: Perennial, occasionally annual, flowering September to March
Ecology: Grows well in shady places, especially under a canopy of trees and in damp fertile sandy loam or clay soils along riverine habitats
Nutritional value: Highly palatable and exceptionally high grazing value persisting well into the cold dry season; particularly attractive to buffalo, waterbuck, hippo, elephant, impala and wildebeest; its seed- grain is consumed by a variety of birds and insects, and by local communities in times of famine
Other features: Drought resistant, may be successfully cultivated

19 Panicum repens L.
Couch Panicum

Description: Medium, tufted, culms erect, creeping rhizomes; inflorescence is partially contracted panicle, leaves pointed and sharp
Habit: Perennial, rhizomatous hydrophyte, flowering October to May
Ecology: Grows in or around permanent or seasonally inundated habitats (fresh or brackish), usually on alluvial sandy or sandy loam soils

Nutritional value: Palatable, good grazing value
Other features: Good soil stabilizer in natural grassland habitats; pioneer grass on newly constructed fish-ponds and dams, and may be cultivated from cuttings for pasture

20 Phragmites australis (Cav.) Trin. ex Steud. (*Katete, Matete*)
Common reed

Description: Very tall, robust reed-grass, extensive creeping rhizomes in dense stands of erect unbranched culms; large fluffy white paniculate inflorescences of silky hispid spikelets
Habit: Perennial, rhizomatous hydrophyte, flowering December to May
Ecology: Grows in aquatic habitats of permanent or seasonally flooded rivers and lagoons of the valley; dense stands provide important habitats for a variety of birds and other aquatic and semi- aquatic fauna
Nutritional value: Low grazing value
Other features: Good soil stabilizer especially in areas liable to flooding; widely used for minor construction, fencing, thatching, mats, baskets

21 Sorghum versicolor Andersson **(***Mulu, Kaemena, Kandodo)*
Black seed sorghum

Description: Medium-tall, tufted, loose culms, nodes have conspicuous rings of long silky white hairs; striking-looking large paniculate inflorescences, slender branchlets, spikelets are brown, hispid, seeds turn glossy black when mature; awns are long (25 - 40 mm) and crinkled; leaves hispid and tapering
Habit: Annual, flowering December to May
Ecology: Prefers wet areas and flourishes in the valley on the ubiquitous water-logged black cotton soil clay areas
Nutritional value: Palatable, but limited grazing value due to poor leaf production, and which may produce prussic acid, poisonous to wildlife and most grazing livestock; seeds are harvested and pounded into porridge in the same way as cultivated Sorghum (*S. bicolor*) and Pearl Millet (*Pennisetum glaucum*) during periods of famine in the valley

Other features: Often grows in association with *Oryza* spp., *Echinochloa colona, Leersia hexandra,* and *Sporobolus pyramidalis* in wetland habitats; apparently contains the Palma-Rosa essential oil; related to cultivated Sorghum *S. bicolor*

22 Sporobolus festivus Hochst. ex A.Rich.
Red dropseed

Description: Small, delicate, tufted, slender culms ascending or erect; "fluffy" inflorescence an open panicle of multiple fine branchlets of pinkish spikelets; leaves sparse, fibrous basal leaf sheaths
Habit: Perennial, flowering December to May
Ecology: Commonly grows in shallow rocky or sandy soil, around poorly-drained seepage areas and roadsides
Nutritional value: Palatable grass, but low leaf production and grazing value
Other features: Useful stabilizer of shallow sandy soils; may be seen along the main game viewing road just after Mfuwe Lodge opposite the old Kakumbi Airstrip short cut

23 Sporobolus panicoides A.Rich.
Famine grass/Christmas tree grass

Description: Medium, sparsely tufted, loose culms, branched; inflorescence an open panicle, whorls of fine branchlets, each with up to 3 large, round orange spikelets when mature; long open leaves, broad base, tapering, serrated margins
Habit: Annual, flowering December to May
Ecology: Pioneer grass of disturbed habitats on a variety of soil types, but prefers sandy, gravelly soils, and light shade
Nutritional value: Low leaf production, poor grazing value, seeds consumed by a variety of birds and insects; seeds may be reaped, pounded and eaten locally during the rains in the absence of millet
Other features: Open panicle of whorled branchlets resemble a "Christmas tree" shape

24 Sporobolus pyramidalis P.Beauv. (*Kalume, Kasepia*)
Catstail dropseed

Description: Medium-tall, densely tufted, erect unbranched culms; long spear-like inflorescence, initially closed panicle, developing into a conical "Christmas tree" or pyramid shape as it opens up; leaves and leaf sheaths glabrous, leaves have distinctive 'hinge' about a third of the way up their length as illustrated, lower leaf sheaths compressed
Habit: Perennial, flowering November to May
Ecology: Widespread on the seasonally waterlogged fringes of dambos and oxbow lagoons; often found in association with *Echinocloa colona, Leersia hexandra,* and *Oryza* spp. dominating the valley floor's floodplains; pioneering grass in periodically flooded watercourses and around dams; grows on all types of soil, especially moist fertile areas of trampled, heavy clay soil; good indicator therefore of trampled or otherwise disturbed habitats, controls soil erosion in disturbed and poorly drained habitats
Nutritional value: Not particularly palatable for grazers, but may be utilised when more palatable species are over-grazed (elephants are fond of it)
Other features: Slender dried culms used to make sweeping brooms

25 Tristachya superba (De Not.) Schweinf. & Aschers. (*Mpolwe*)
Giant trident grass

Description: Tall-very tall, tufted, stout culms from bulbous base and creeping rhizomes; paniculate inflorescence of spreading branches, softly hispid; golden-brown spikelets in triads, rarely in pairs; broad leaves and basal leaf sheaths, softly hispid, clustered around base
Habit: Perennial, flowering late rainy season February to August
Ecology: Widespread in back-country woodlands and dambos of the valley, on a variety of sandy, sandy loam or gravelly soils; fire-resistant
Nutritional value: Poor grazing value, becoming hard and unpalatable as it matures in the dry season; warthogs known to eat its rhizomes
Other features: Hard hollow culms may be used to construct fences and awnings, and as drinking straws

1a Aristida congesta

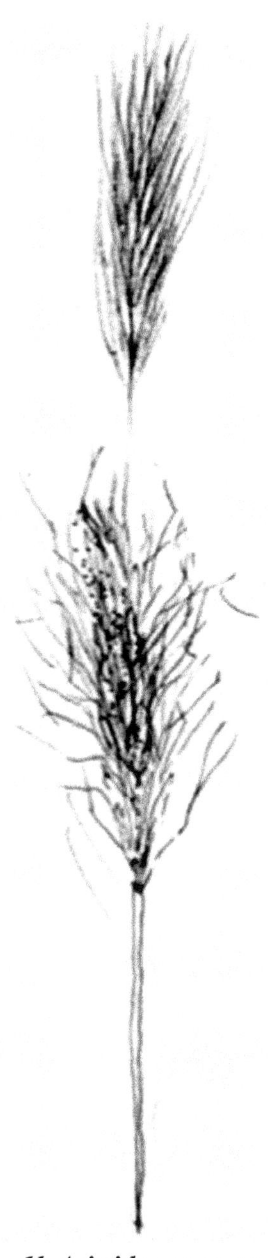

1b Aristida congesta

2a Aristida junciformis

2b Aristida junciformis

3a Aristida rhiniochloa

3b Aristida rhiniochloa

4 Eragrostis aethiopica

5 Eragrostis aspera

6 Eragrostis cilianens

7 Eragrostis ciliaris

8 Eragrostis gangetica

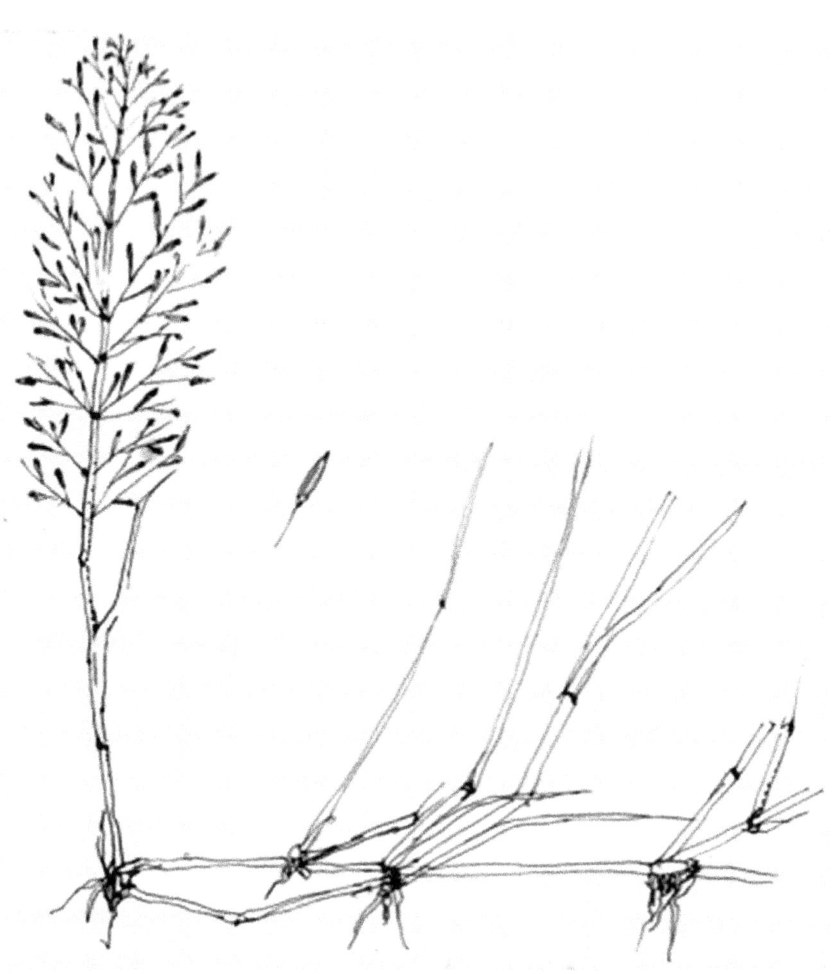

9 Eragrostis trichophora

10 Eragrostis viscosa

11 Imperata cylindrica

12 Leersia hexandra

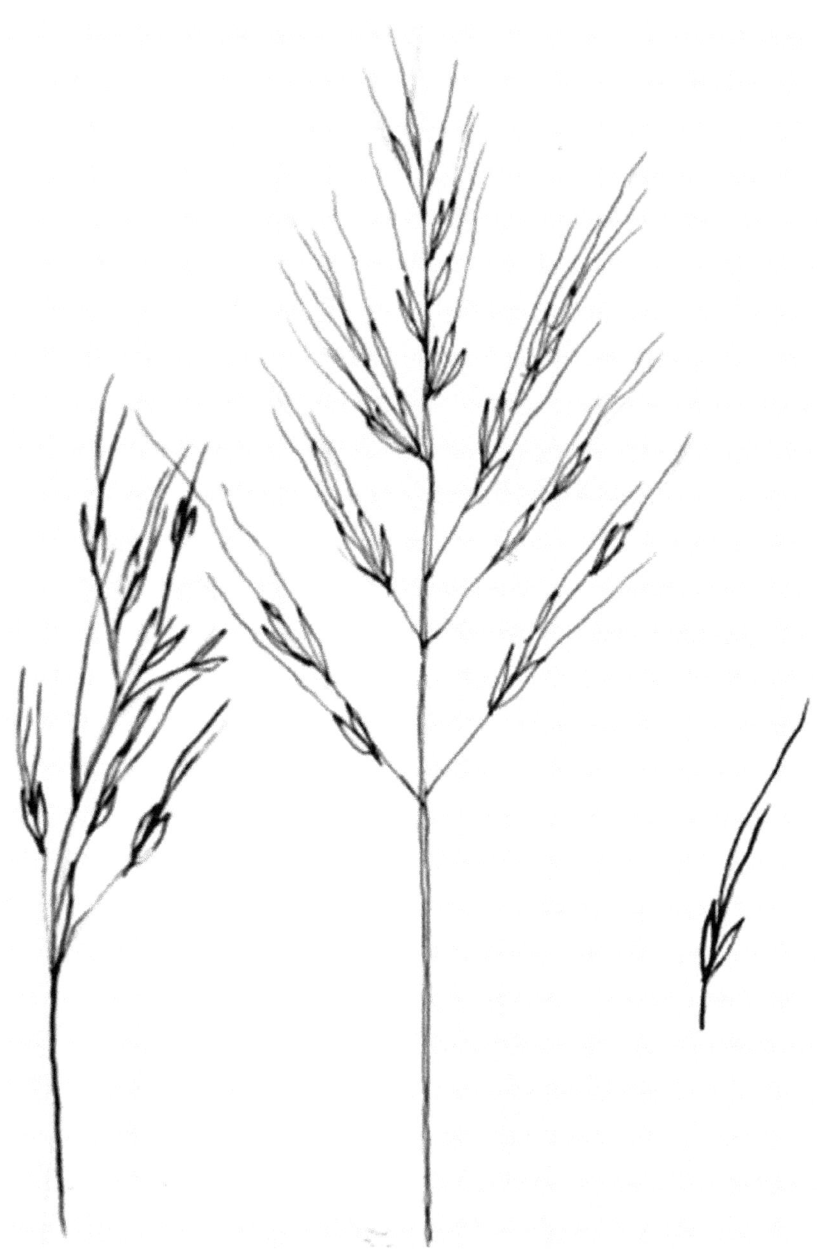

13a Loudetia simplex

13b Loudetia simplex

14 Melinis repens

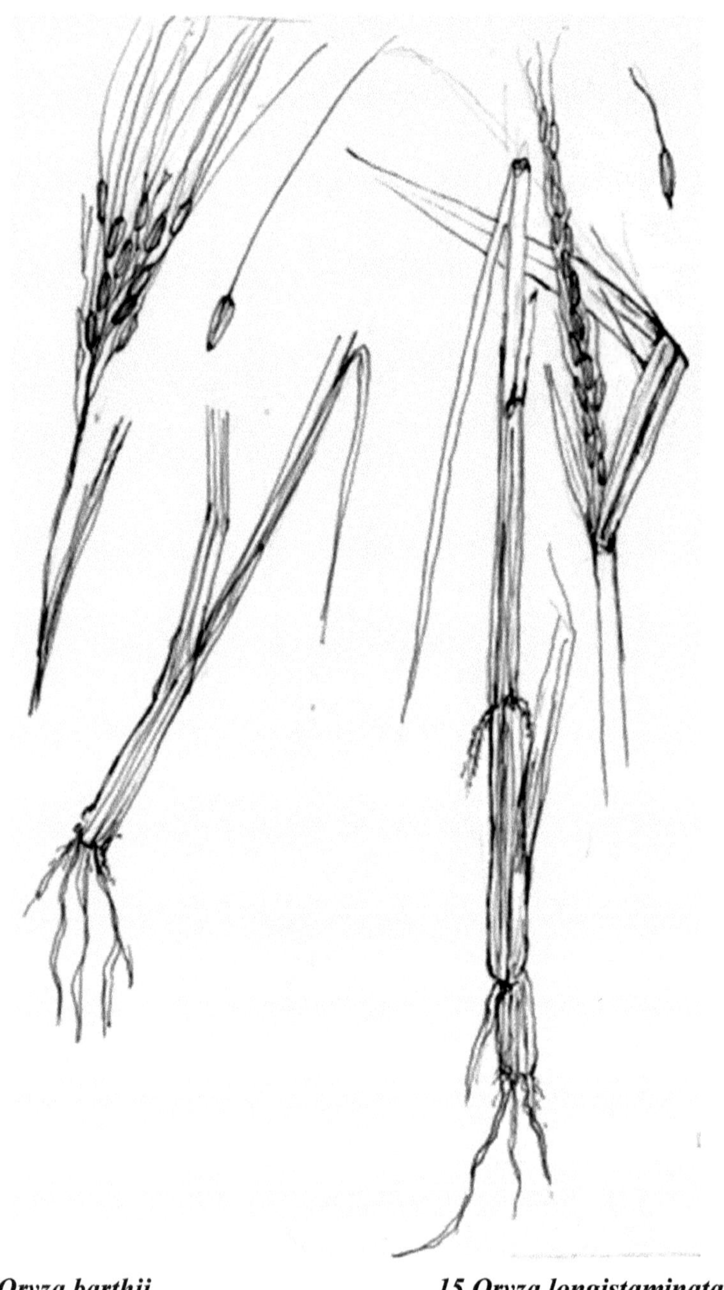

16 Oryza barthii *15 Oryza longistaminata*

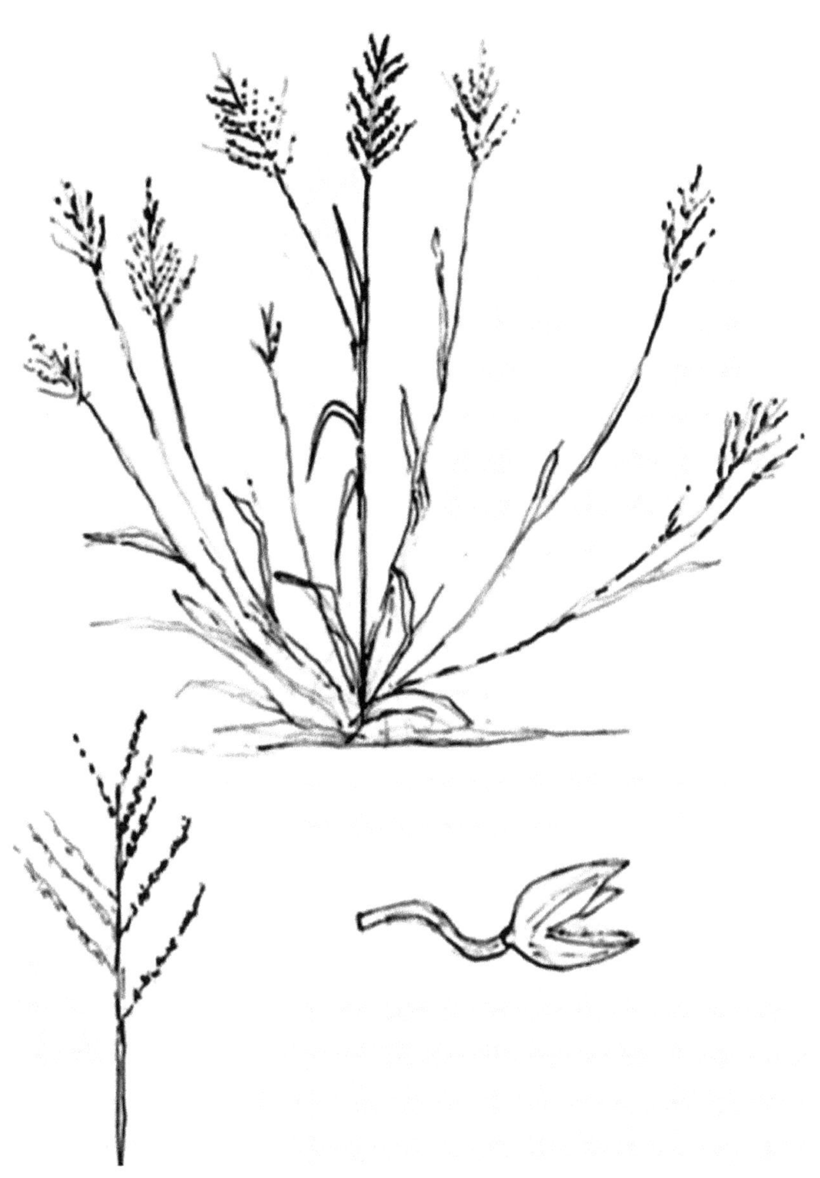

17 Panicum coloratum

18a Panicum maximum

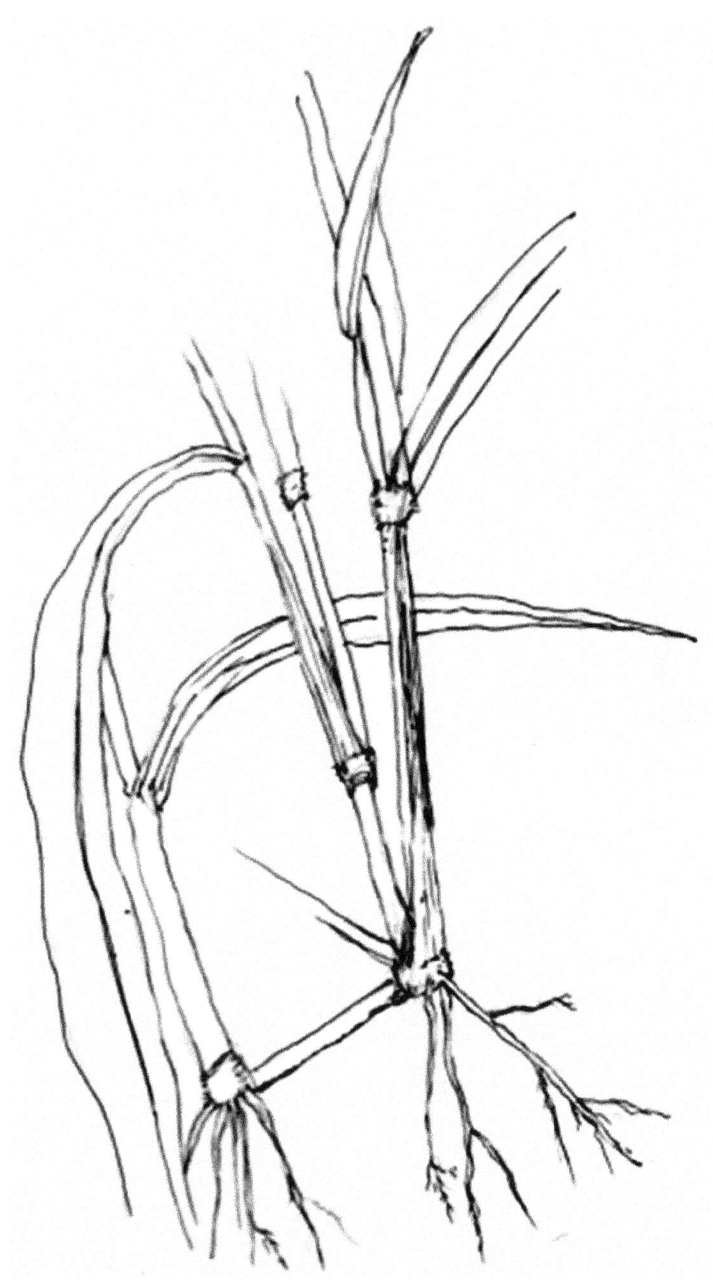

18b Panicum maximum

19 Panicum repens

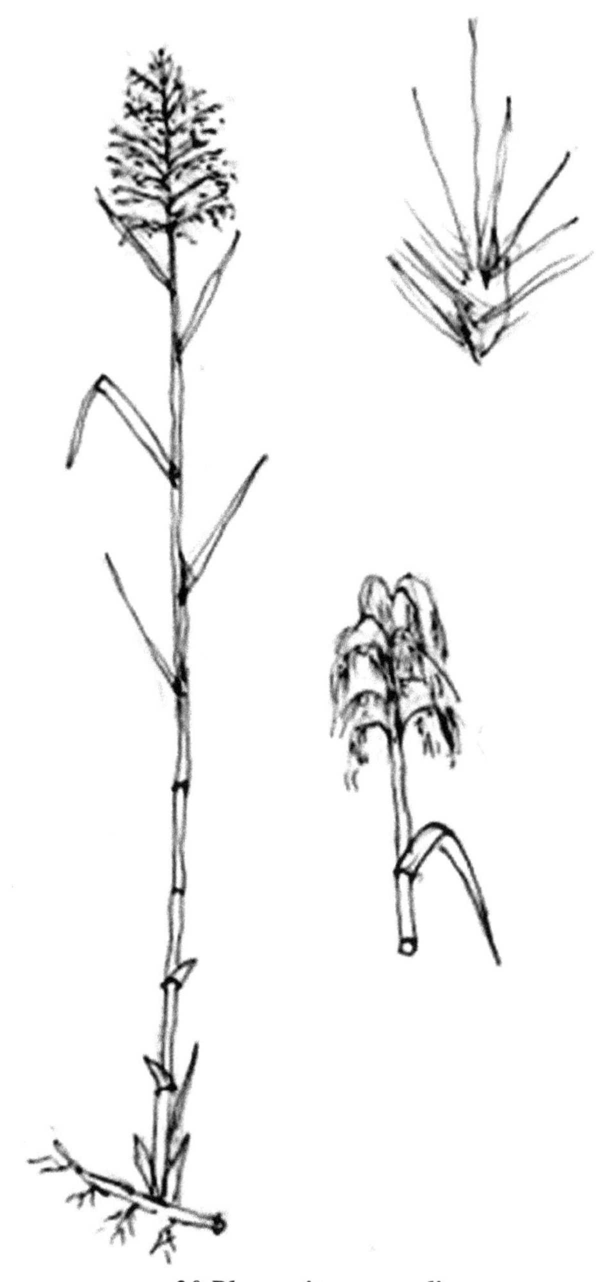

20 Phragmites australis

21 Sorghum versicolor

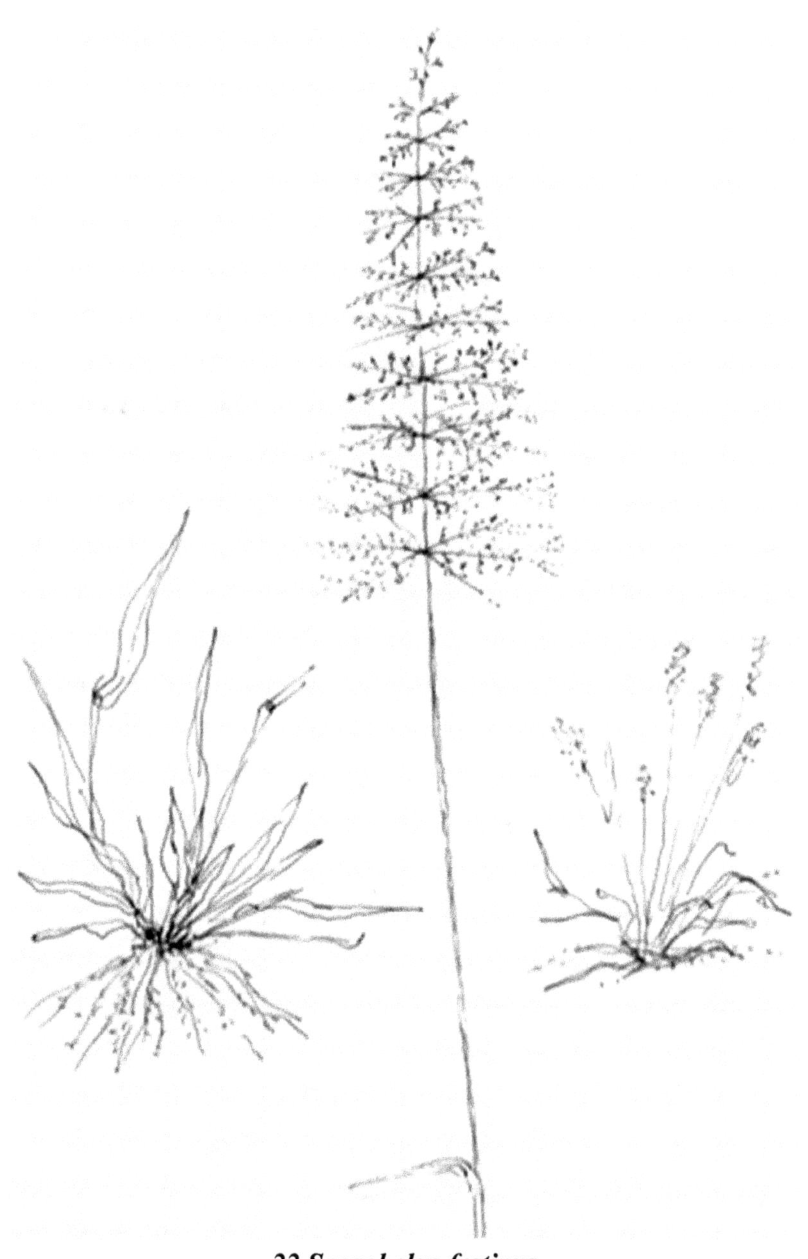

22 Sporobolus festivus

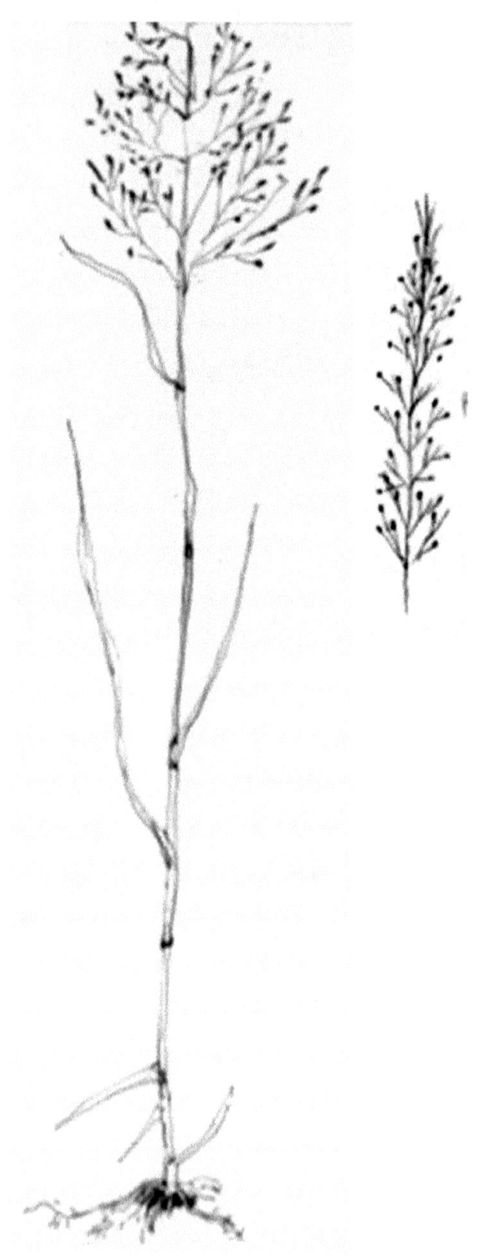

23 Sporobolus panicoides

24a Sporobolus pyramidalis

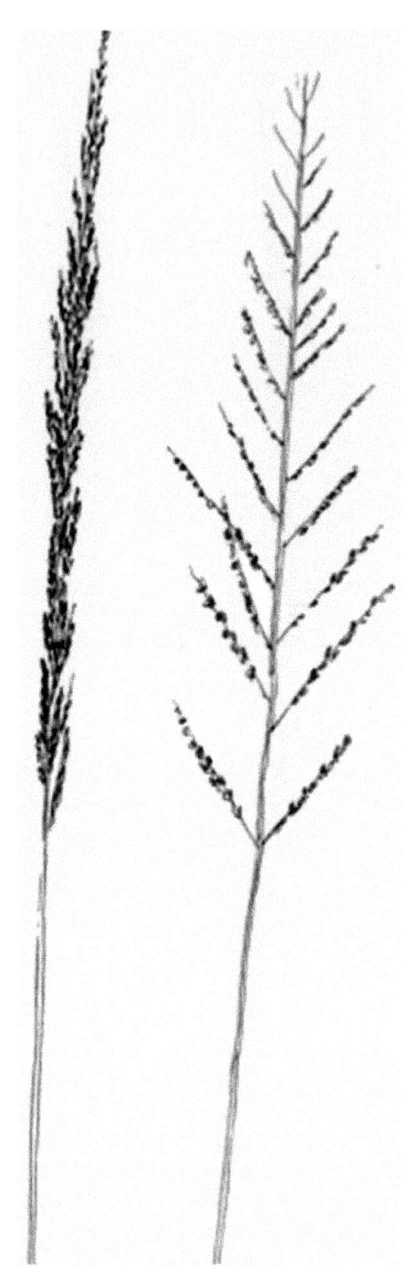

24b Sporobolus pyramidalis

25 Tristachya superba

SOLITARY INFLORESCENCES

26 Cenchrus ciliaris L.
Foxtail buffalo grass

Description: Medium, tufted, culms bending at swollen nodes, branched; inflorescence a single, dense, straw-coloured bristly spike flushed with purple, spikelets drop off in entirety when mature; broad leaves tapering to fine points, ligule inconspicuous
Habit: Perennial, flowering August to April, rhizomatous, deeply rooted
Ecology: Hardy, drought resistant; thrives in warm arid conditions, in stable or disturbed open grassland, on sandy, well-drained soils
Nutritional value: Palatable, good grazing, high leaf production
Other features: Useful stabilizer of disturbed soils; may be cultivated for pasture grazing and hay, sometimes as an ornamental

27 Ctenium concinnum Nees
Sickle grass

Description: Short-medium, densely tufted, culms slender, erect, unbranched; inflorescence grows into a single, one-sided spike, bending over into a sickle shape (crescent moon) and curling when mature; grey-green spikelets, flat with long straight awns (4.5 - 5.5 mm); thin wiry leaves clustered at base, fibrous leaf sheaths; ligule a short membrane
Habit: Perennial, flowering December to April
Ecology: Climax grass of open or woodland grasslands, in dry or moist sandy soil
Nutritional value: Hard, unpalatable, poor grazing value
Other features: Resilient grass often seen on roadsides

28 Heteropogon contortus (L.) P.Beauv. ex Roem. & Schult.
Spear grass

Description: Medium, tufted, culms may branch into individual spikes from upper nodes; inflorescence a single green raceme; green spikelets with fluffy white hairs, and long velvety brown awns (50 - 80 mm) which twist and tangle into knots as they mature; basal leaves and leaf sheaths compressed; leaves often folded, may be blunt-tipped, glabrous

Habit: Perennial, flowering October to June

Ecology: Widespread climax grass growing readily in a variety of habitats, particularly hillsides and disturbed habitats such as roadsides, in gravelly, well-drained soils of various types

Nutritional value: Palatable, good grazing value but only in the early growing season for many grazers (especially zebra and waterbuck), soon becoming hard and unpalatable

Other features: Upon maturity, the long black awns dry out and crinkle, twisting themselves into a zig-zag disarray of tangled clusters, aptly representing their specific Latin name, *contortus;* when wet the dried out awns "animate" twisting and driving their seeds into the ground; the spear-like awns can also penetrate the pelage of livestock and wildlife, causing irritation, physical damage and injury

29 Rottboellia cochinchinensis (Lour.) Clayton Synonym *R. exaltata (Zuya)*
Itch grass

Description: Tall-very tall, tufted, robust, erect, long culms, typically branching from stilt roots; inflorescence inconspicuous single cylindrical raceme, glabrous; spikelets sunken into pedicels; leaves broad, long, rough, tapering; basal leaf sheaths covered with harsh, prickly, irritant hairs, short membranous ligule

Habit: Annual, flowering December to June; forms dense stands on stilt roots

Ecology: Growing in wooded grassland and along roadsides and disturbed habitats, often in shade on damp black cotton soil **Nutritional value**: Good foraging grass but unpleasant to handle due to its hard, sharp hairs; seeds favoured by guinea fowls, helping dispersal

Other features: Increasingly problematic weed of cultivation; seedlings recognised by their unusual seeds that often remain attached when up-rooted

30 Setaria incrassata (Hochst.) Hack. *(Kasense)*
Vlei bristle grass

Description: Small, densely tufted, lower culms pinkish, erect, nodes hairy; inflorescence a dense erect single spike-like panicle, spikelets greenish to bristly yellow; leaves broad, blue-green, prominent mid-rib
Habit: Perennial, flowering October to May; rhizomatous
Ecology: grows in a variety of habitats, but prefers damp fertile black clay soils in areas such as dambos, riverbanks and down-slope seepages
Nutritional value: Palatable, good leaf production and grazing value
Other features: Useful for binding damp soil, limiting erosion; commonly used locally to thatch houses because although the stems are not ideal the broad flat leaves (up to 14 mm wide) create a waterproofing in a way that the various species of local *Hyparrhenia* cannot do (*Hyparrhenia* leaves have to be 'combed' or stripped which is labour intensive and not that effective because the stems are thick and porous); there are fine stands of *kasense* that may be seen in the low-lying areas on the right-hand side of the bridge at the main entrance to the SLNP; this is one of the areas where women traditionally harvest the grass annually for thatching the roofs of their houses

31 Setaria pallide-fusca (Schumach.) Stapf & C.E.Hubb. *(Mpukusa)*
Garden bristle grass

Description: Small-medium, loosely tufted, culms branched, sometimes bending, nodes glabrous; inflorescence un-branched spike-like panicle; green spikelets, with yellow, orange, brown, purple-brown bristles; leaves, red highlights, contracted around culms, glabrous, leaf sheaths compressed
Habit: Annual, flowering December to April
Ecology: Grows in most soil types, favours damp, disturbed soils, tolerates shade
Nutritional value: Average palatability, but low leaf production and grazing value
Other features: Readily colonizes bare soil, limiting soil erosion; villagers twist this grass into cord for binding grain sheaves

32 ***Setaria sphacelata (Schumach.) Stapf & C.E.Hubb. ex Moss*** (spp. *Mpukusa, Kasense, Lubemba, Muchila wa numbu)* Common bristle grass (*var. sphacelata*)

Description: Medium-tall, densely tufted, culms erect, nodes glabrous; inflorescence unbranched spike-like panicle with greenish spikelets and yellow bristles; leaves and basal leaf sheaths glabrous; clustered around base
Habit: Perennial, flowering October to June, rhizomatous
Ecology: Grows in a wide range of open grassland habitats and damp but well-drained sandy soils, often on moist disturbed soils, and hill slopes' seepages
Nutritional value: palatable, good leaf production and grazing value; seed-grain consumed by birds and insects
Other features: Binds damp soil, limiting erosion; there are many varieties of *S. sphacelata*, most may be cultivated for pasture and hay; extensive stands found in dambo areas of the valley providing valuable grazing for elephants and other grazing animals

26 Cenchrus ciliaris

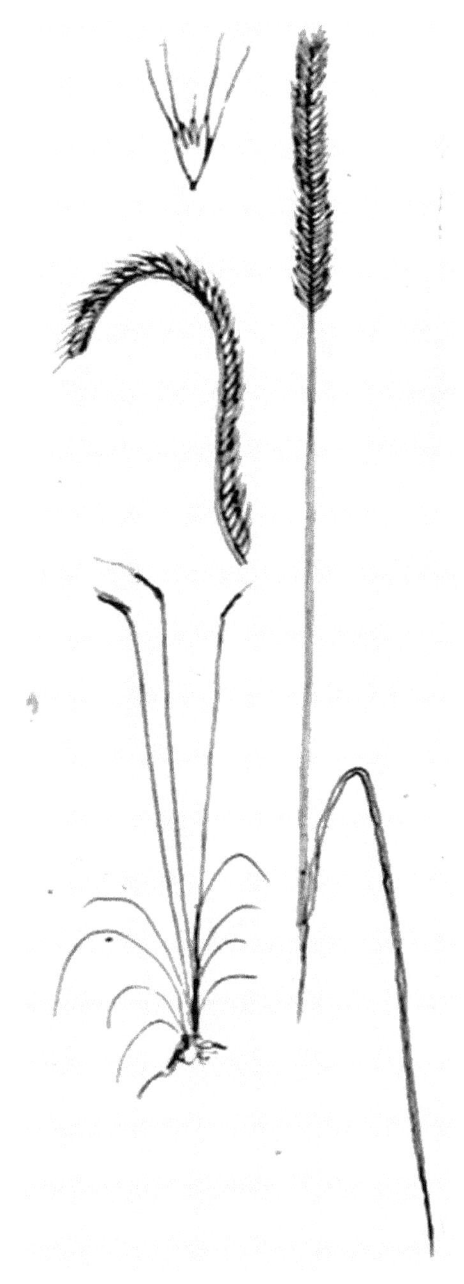

27 Ctenium concinnum

28a Heteropogon contortus

28b Heteropogon contortus

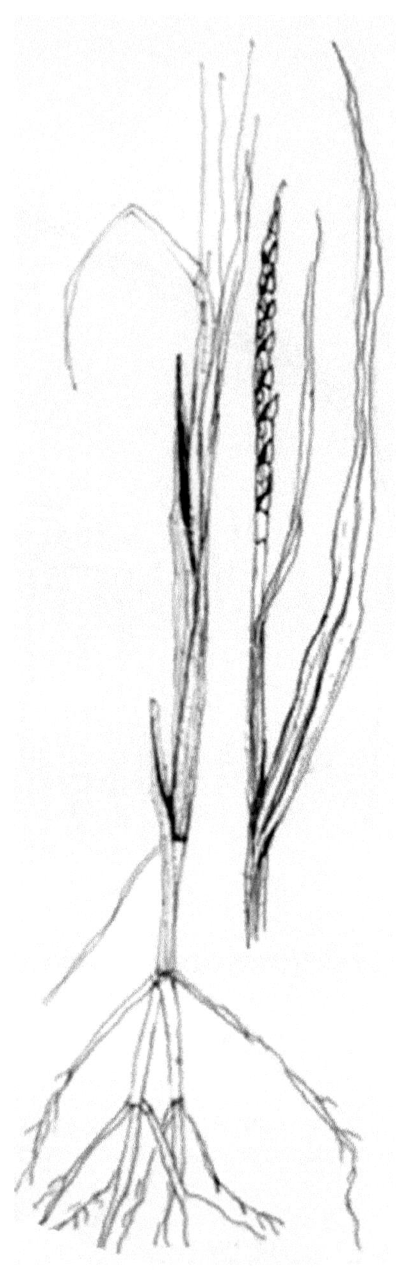

29 Rottboellia cochinchinensis

30 Setaria incrassata

31 Setaria pallide-fusca

32a Setaria sphacelata

32b Setaria sphacelata

FALSE PANICLE INFLORESCENCES

33 Andropogon eucomus Nees
Snowflake grass

Description: Medium-tall, tufted, short rhizomes; culms erect, reddish; inflorescence 2 to 5 fluffy, silvery white racemes, hairy, each spikelet with single long straight awn (7 - 22 mm); leaves clustered around base, basal leaf sheaths compressed
Habit: Perennial, flowering November to May
Ecology: Grows in wet, poorly drained areas such as dambos and seepages, often on disturbed sandy soils
Nutritional value: Unpalatable, low grazing value
Other features: Stabiliser of disturbed moist soils, indicator of poor drainage

34 Cymbopogon caesius (Hook. & Arn.) Stapf (*Museye)*
Broad-leaved turpentine grass

Description: Tall, densely tufted, culms erect, usually unbranched; distinctive inflorescence of paired racemes with right-angled arrangement on the stem; awns fairly long and twisted (7 - 19.5 mm), glabrous; leaves very broad from base, tapering, bright green, prominent mid-rib, sometimes waxy, inconspicuous ligule; as its common name implies this grass is strongly aromatic, smelling like turpentine
Habit: Perennial, flowering November to May
Ecology: Grows in most open habitats and soil types, but particularly on sandy, gravelly soils in disturbed habitats
Nutritional value: Aromatic and unpalatable, therefore limited grazing value, one of the last species to be utilised at the very end of the dry season
Other features: May be used for thatching; contains essential oils giving its turpentine or citronella aroma; may be used to deter pests such as rodents and insects; similar species include *C. plurinodis* (smaller leaves, less bright green, concentrated around base of culms), and *C. validus* (very tall, purple-brown inflorescence, prominent

ligule); in form and appearance may be confused with *Hyparrhenia* spp. which however are hairy and not distinctly aromatic

35 Hemarthria altissima (Poir.) Stapf & C.E.Hubb.
Swamp couch

Description: Medium-tall culms, reddish-brown, creeping rhizomes; inflorescences compressed racemes indistinct from culms, sunken spikelets; leaves also reddish-brown, twisted when drying out, basal leaf sheaths strongly compressed
Habit: Perennial, flowering November to May, rhizomatous **Ecology**: Aquatic grass growing in dambos and swampy areas, in most soil types **Nutritional value**: Palatable, high leaf production and grazing value; rhizomes are nutritious
Other features: May be used as cultivated pasture; rhizomes may be eaten raw

Thatching grasses

The next four species that all grow in the valley are known as "thatching grasses" with thick stems that are not all that waterproof; the last three are coarser than the fine thatching grass *Hyparrhenia filipendula*, although ecologically they may all occur together in the same habitat; these thatching grasses usually require 'combing' or the removal of the leaves before they are really suitable for thatch in which case the stems are bundled and bound together in small sections; they are therefore not used locally as much as the traditional finer-stemmed *kasense* or *Setaria incrassata* thatching grass which is favoured by villagers for its waterproof quality.

36 Hyparrhenia filipendula (Hochst.) Stapf *(*spp. *Kavimbamkutu* spp. *Lupala, Numbu, Nkoche)*
Fine thatching grass

Description: Medium-tall, moderately tufted, culms flexible; inflorescence finely branched, loosely spreading panicle, light green

short racemes in pairs, each with one or two long, thin brown awns (30 - 55 mm); leaves finer than other thatching grasses
Habit: Perennial, flowering November to April
Ecology: Common in riverine grasslands, open dry areas and often along roadsides
Nutritional value: Average palatability and grazing when young and succulent but soon becomes hard and fibrous, although elephants do utilise it in this form
Other features: Popular thatching grass

37 Hyparrhenia hirta (L.) Stapf
Common thatching grass

Description: Medium, moderately tufted, culms erect; inflorescence contracted, erect pairs of racemes, spikelets hairy whitish with hairy brown awns (10 - 35 mm); culms and leaves may be flushed red early in the growing season
Habit: Perennial, flowering September to March
Ecology: Common in riverine grasslands, open dry areas and often along roadsides
Nutritional value: Average palatability and grazing when young and succulent but soon becomes hard and fibrous, although elephants do utilise it in this form
Other features: Popular thatching grass

38 Hyparrhenia rufa (Nees) Stapf
Giant thatching grass

Description: Very tall, robust, densely tufted, culms erect, usually unbranched; inflorescence contracted sometimes lax, multiple pairs of racemes, spikelets also in pairs, hairy whitish with long twisted yellow-brown awns (20 - 30 mm), may change in colour through the season from yellowish to reddish-brown; culms and leaves may be flushed red early in the growing season, leaves broad, leaf sheaths glabrous, ligule a firm brown membrane
Habit: Perennial or annual; flowering December to June; rhizomatous (short)

Ecology: Common in moist clay or sandy loam soils of dambos and riverine grasslands, sometimes in drier open areas, along roadsides and other disturbed areas; pyrophyte
Nutritional value: Average palatability and grazing when young and succulent, soon becoming hard, fibrous, although elephants may still utilise it
Other features: With its large, coarse, hard stems, this thatching grass is not as waterproof as finer-stemmed thatching grasses

39 Hyperthelia dissoluta (Nees ex Steud.) Clayton
Yellow thatching grass

Description: Medium-tall, robustly tufted, culms erect, usually unbranched, yellow; inflorescence long vertically contracted racemes and spikelets, green, with long robust yellow awns (50 - 100 mm); leaves green, leaf sheaths with prominent auricles; entire plant appears yellowish-green
Habit: Perennial, flowering all year but predominantly December to June
Ecology: Common in riverine grasslands and fertile valley soils, as well as open dry areas, often along roadsides and other disturbed habitats
Nutritional value: Average palatability and grazing when young and succulent but soon becomes hard and fibrous, although elephants do utilise it in this form
Other features: Popular thatching grass, but coarser than *H.filipendula*

40 Andropogon gayanus Kunth *(Nyamalokoto)*
Blue grass

Description: Medium-tall, tufted, hardy; culms erect, unbranched, "waxy" blue-green appearance; inflorescence develops into two finger-like racemes raised on top of the stalk about 5 to 10 cm long, slightly hairy, 2 to 3 long slightly crinkled awns (13 - 32 mm); leaves may be flushed dark reddish or purple, narrow at the base almost to prominent mid-rib, basal leaf sheaths compressed

Habit: Perennial, flowering December to May or later
Ecology: Adaptable, growing in a wide range of habitats and soil types often high in magnesium; prefers shady, broken terrain
Nutritional value: Palatable and good grazing in early growing season when nutritious forage value highest
Other features: Before its inflorescences appear stands of this tallish grass look like a *Hyparrhenia* sp because of the height and coarseness of its stems and leaves

33 Andropogon eucomus

34 Cymbopogon caesius

35 Hemarthria altissima

36 Hyparrhenia filipendula

37 Hyparrhenia hirta

38 Hyparrhenia rufa

39 Hyperthelia dissoluta

40 Andropogon gayanus

DIGITATE INFLORESCENCES

41 Bothriochloa insculpta (Hochst. ex A.Rich.) A.Camus
Pin hole grass

Description: Medium, tufted, culms erect, nodes dark with conspicuous ring of white hairs; purple semi-digitate inflorescence, 5- 10 racemes loosely ascending or erect, spikelets with small pits and long sometimes tangled awns (15 - 25 mm); blue-green leaves, lower with spreading white hairs
Habit: Perennial, flowering October to June; may be stoloniferous
Ecology: Favours open stable or disturbed grasslands, hillsides and gullies on moist and well drained soils
Nutritional value: Birds do eat the seed, but it is unpalatable to grazers due to the aromatic oils it contains
Other features: The pin hole name refers to tiny pits visible on its spikelets

42 Chloris virgata Sw. *(Nkombwa)*
Feather-top chloris

Description: Short-medium, weakly tufted, culms loosely erect, rooting at lower nodes, may be stoloniferous; digitate inflorescence, erect, contracted 4-12 racemes, feathery white hairy spikelets, seeds turning black when mature; leaves folded open, prominent mid-rib, pointed and may be serrated, upper leaf sheaths may be inflated, lower compressed
Habit: Annual, occasionally perennial, flowering December to June
Ecology: Commonly grows on old cultivated and disturbed lands in a variety of soil types but favours clay soils on the edges of seasonally inundated dambos and grassland
Nutritional value: Average leaf production, but palatable and valuable grazing in the absence of perennials
Other features: Well-known weed on cultivated croplands, but otherwise can be a valuable pioneering grass, although due to its palatability is easily over-grazed leaving exposed soil susceptible to erosion

43 Chloris gayana Kunth
Rhodes grass

Description: Medium, tufted, culms loosely ascending or erect; digitate inflorescence, 4-11 racemes loosely whorled (whorls may be paired) but curling up and inwards after the light brown spikelets have dropped; leaves smooth, folded open, basal leaf sheaths compressed
Habit: Perennial, flowering November to May, strongly stoloniferous
Ecology: Naturally uncommon, growing in loamy soils on the edges of seasonally inundated dambos and grassland, but improved cultivars are widespread and grow well in most soil types and damp or irrigated habitats
Nutritional value: High leaf production, palatability and grazing value, especially early in the growth season
Other features: Popular cultivated pasture, excellent grazing and hay; easy to establish, resilient to grazing pressure, good soil stabilizer; cultivated Katambora strain resistant to root-knot nematodes and frost

44 Cynodon dactylon (L.) Pers. *(Kapinga)*
Couch grass

Description: Short, creeping grass spreading from stolons and underground rhizomes, culms prostrate, loosely ascending to erect peduncles; digitate inflorescence, 3-7 racemes loosely whorled, spikelets flat, awnless; leaves glabrous bending at right angles to leaf sheaths, pointing upwards from horizontal mat-forming stems
Habit: Perennial, creeping, strongly stoloniferous and rhizomatous; flowering September to May
Ecology: Widespread, growing readily in a variety of soils on the edges of seasonally inundated dambos, grasslands, and damp disturbed and even over-grazed areas
Nutritional value: Low leaf production, but palatable and good grazing, staying green until late in the dry season
Other features: Commonly seen in dried out lagoon beds being grazed by large aggregations of puku; a popular cultivated pasture, excellent grazing and hay; hardy lawn grass, easy to establish, resilient to grazing pressure, good soil stabilizer, often used on sports fields and in gardens due to its good ground coverage

45 Dactyloctenium aegyptium (L.) Willd. (*Kambusa, Chimbusa)*
Common crowfoot

Description: Short, loosely tufted, rooting from lower nodes, culms bending, spreading, ascending to peduncles; digitate inflorescence, 3-7 (commonly 4) thick horizontally arranged racemes (one-sided spikes) like helicopter rotor blades, but often unequal in length; leaves flat with lightly hairy margins, prominent mid-rib, leaf sheaths compressed, membranous ligule with short hairs
Habit: Annual, flowering January to April, rooting from lower nodes (not stolons or rhizomes)
Ecology: Grows in most soil types, preferring sandy soils in disturbed areas where water collects, such as on cultivated lands, gardens and roadsides
Nutritional value: Palatable, but leaf production and grazing value low value
Other features: Pioneering grass colonising disturbed areas; seeds eaten by villagers in times of famine, and used as traditional medicine to treat kidney ailments and coughing; dry seeds dispersed by wind, birds and animals; bruised young seeds may be used as a fish poison

46 Dacytloctenium giganteum B.S.Fisher & Schweick.
Giant crowfoot

Description: Medium, robust, tufted sometimes in dense stands, culms bending from lower nodes, ascending becoming erect; digitate inflorescence, 3-8 (commonly 6) thick horizontally arranged racemes (one-sided spikes) with reddish-brown spikelets and short hair-like awns (2.5 - 9 mm), tending to curl upwards when the seeds have dropped; leaves folded open with lightly hairy margins, prominent mid-rib, leaf sheaths compressed, membranous ligule with short hairs
Habit: Annual, flowering October to June
Ecology: Grows in most soil types, but preferring sandy soils such as sandy riverbanks, and in disturbed areas where water collects such as on cultivated lands and roadsides
Nutritional value: Palatable, high leaf production, good grazing especially for zebra and waterbuck

Other features: Pioneering grass readily colonising large areas of bare sandy soil

47 Digitaria diagonalis (Nees) Stapf
Brown seed finger grass

Description: Medium, tightly tufted, culms erect, unbranched, bulbous and hairy at base, nodes purplish with white hairs; semi-digitate inflorescence, numerous (10-30) ascending or erect racemes on long central axis, singly or in whorls, spikelets, may be hairy, in groups (3-6), seeds shiny brownish; leaves glabrous, prominent mid-rib, leaf sheaths hairy, fibrous at base, ligule irregular rim of hairs
Habit: Perennial, flowering December to April
Ecology: Grows in open grassland and savanna, preferring moist, sandy well-drained soils
Nutritional value: Good leaf production, but hard, unpalatable, low grazing value
Other features: Desirable climax grass for grassland stability

48 Digitaria milanjiana (Rendle) Stapf (spp. *Lwiwa, Rwiwa)*
Mlanje finger grass

Description: Medium, loosely tufted, culms ascending erect, unbranched, bulbous and hairy at base, nodes dark, usually glabrous; semi-digitate inflorescence, numerous (2-18) ascending or erect racemes on long central axis, singly or in whorls, spikelets, may be lightly hairy, in groups (3-6), seeds shiny brownish; leaves glabrous or lightly hairy, leaf sheaths hairy and fibrous at base, membranous ligule
Habit: Perennial, flowering January to February, rhizomatous, branching, sometimes stoloniferous
Ecology: Grows in dambos, floodplains and also in disturbed areas, preferring moist, loamy or heavy clay soils
Nutritional value: Good leaf production, palatable but hard, average grazing value
Other features: Readily seeded as pasture

49 Echinochloa colona (L.) Link (*Chipunga Malyamvuwu, Lupunga, Chikwanje)*
Jungle rice

Description: Short-medium, tufted, culms branched, ascending erect, rooting from bent lower nodes; elongate digitate inflorescence, 8 or more racemes in alternate pairs, ascending, spikelets in 4 rows on axes, lightly hairy, awnless, green to purple; leaves glabrous, may have purple bars, no ligule; when seen together in an expansive stand the leaves appear from a distance to be more of a yellow ochre than green **Habit**: Annual, flowering January to April
Ecology: Semi-aquatic grass, growing in muddy swampy places in or near water; in drier areas will still propagate from lower-lying nodes rooting on the ground
Nutritional value: Palatable, good grazing, and grain is eaten by birds; people in the valley still collect the grain as a nutritious food-source in times of famine
Other features: At the height of its maturity in the rains, this grass forms a broad sweep of purple heads in its aquatic habitats, often in association with *Oyrza barthii*; examples of fine stands of this attractive grass are to be found at Lupunga spur, Mopani spur and the open flooded areas around Mfuwe Lodge; dried seeds may be pounded or even milled, like cultivated sorghum or pearl millet, and made into *nshima* in the normal way and tasting delicious, somewhat oilier than cultivated sorghum or millet grown by local farmers

50 Eleusine africana Kenn.-O'Bryne, Synonym *E. coracana subsp. africana; E. indica subsp. africana* (*Bule, dulu)*
Goose grass (finger millet)

Description: Short-medium, partly prostrate, robust, tufted, strongly rooted, culms flattened, slanted or ascending; semi-digitate inflorescence, 3-10 racemes in whorls of alternate pairs, sometimes singly below whorl, ascending, spikelets in rows underneath racemes' axes, awnless, glabrous or lightly hairy; leaves glabrous, strongly keeled, blunt-tipped, hairy membranous ligule, basal leaf sheaths compressed, hairy

Habit: Annual or perennial, flowering November to February
Ecology: Grows in all soil types, favours rocky or turf soils
Nutritional value: Average to good grazing, nutritious seeds used as grain by local communities in times of famine; cultivated varieties historically provided a staple grain in Africa, and were exported to India
Other features: Mature grass not easily removed due to well-developed rooting system; the whole plant, especially the root, is used in traditional medicine as a diuretic, anthelminthic, diaphoretic and febrifuge and for treating coughs and other ailments; known to have anti-oxidant and anti-inflammatory properties; however, may contain hydrogen cyanide leading to deaths in livestock, especially the young

51 Eriochloa stapfiana Clayton
Harpoon grass

Description: Medium, robust, tufted, culms ascending erect, rooting from bent lower nodes; elongated digitate inflorescence, 6-many racemes usually alternate but may be in pairs, bearing spikelets in pairs or on short appressed side branchlets, may be lightly hairy, awnless; leaves open, usually glabrous, lower glume absent or obscure membranous ligule
Habit: Perennial, flowering October to May
Ecology: Semi-aquatic, grows along riverbanks and riverbeds, in sandy or clay soils, near or in water, culms often floating
Nutritional value: high leaf production, palatable, good grazing **Other features**: Binds and stabilizes riverbanks and riverbeds from erosion; intergrades with *E. meyerana* which is smaller but otherwise almost indistinguishable; associates with *Echinochloa colona* in waterlogged areas, with which its inflorescence may be confused, especially when both are in a mature state of red or purple inflorescences

52 Oplismenus hirtellus (L.) P.Beauv.
Basket grass

Description: Short, creeping sometimes climbing, culms rooting at nodes, spaced digitate inflorescence, partially ascending alternately in 2-8 clusters (racemes) of 1-10 purple spikelets with short sticky awns (3 - 14 mm)

Habit: Perennial; flowering January to June
Ecology: Grows in damp, cool, shady woodland or forest floors
Nutritional value: Low leaf production and bulk, poor grazing value
Other features: Often the only grass able to grow in damp, deep shade

53 Pogonarthria squarrosa (Licht.) Pilg. (*Kasense)* Herringbone grass

Description: Medium, tufted, culms erect, unbranched, entire plant is usually glabrous; elongated digitate inflorescence multiple light brown racemes horizontally whorled and ascending becoming darker to purple with maturity; rows of small solitary spikelets under racemes, light brown/red, awnless; leaves flat, rolled when mature **Habit**: Perennial, flowering February to March in the valley **Ecology**: Prefers poor sandy soils but found in most parts of the valley **Nutritional value**: Unpalatable, low leaf production and grazing value
Other features: Its common name, Herringbone grass, relates to resemblance of the inflorescence to a fish bone with its ribs off the central spine; may be confused with *Sporobolus pyramidalis* but differs in that the herringbone appearance of *Pogonarthria squarrosa* is more defined with a thicker ribbed section, each spike being sickle-shaped, whereas the spikes of *Sporobolus pyramidalis* are finer and branch off the main stem at a straighter angle; dried culms may be bound together and used as hand brooms

54 Setaria homonyma (Steud.) Chiov.
Fan leaf "timothy"

Description: Short, sparsely tufted, culms bent, branched, rooting from lower nodes; elongated digitate inflorescence 6-10 racemes, spikelets in 2 rows, each with single bristle (5 - 10 mm); leaves bright light green, wide, pleated, finely hairy
Habit: Annual, flowering January to February **Ecology**: Thrives in shady damp, clay soils of riverine woodlands and forests
Nutritional value: Palatable, but low leaf production and grazing value
Other features: Useful grazing in absence of other grasses and binds damp soil in deep shade

55 Trichoneura grandiglumis (Nees) Ekman
Small rolling grass

Description: Short-medium, sparsely tufted, culms erect or ascending; semi-digitate inflorescence, 10-20 racemes at right angles in gently ascending whorl, spikelets separated alternately in 2 rows, long sharp glumes; leaves may be hairy and rolled or expanded, membranous ligule
Habit: Perennial, flowering December to January
Ecology: Grows in sandy soils of a variety of grassland and savanna habitats, a sub climax grass of disturbed areas
Nutritional value: Unpalatable, low leaf production and grazing value
Other features: Inflorescence breaks off at maturity and rolls in the wind dispersing its seeds

56 Urochloa mosambicensis (Hack.) Dandy (*Nagapanda)*
Signal grass

Description: Medium, tufted, entire plant hairy, culms ascending, bending, usually rooting and branching from lower nodes, distinct ring of hairs on nodes; spaced digitate inflorescence, 4- 12 racemes alternately horizontally ascending like "railway signals", spikelets with short awns sharply pointed, in 2 alternate rows; leaves pale green, short, broad, wavy margins,
rounded base, basal leaf sheaths may be hairy, ligule a hairy membrane
Habit: Perennial, flowering October to May, stoloniferous or more rarely rhizomatous
Ecology: Grows in most soil types, but favours fertile, well-drained sandy loam, tolerates shade, often growing in sheltered disturbed habitats
Nutritional value: Palatable, good grazing retaining its nutritious value well into the dry season
Other features: Utilised by hippo, warthog and antelopes; may be grown and cultivated from seed

41a Bothriochloa insculpta

41b Bothriochloa insculpta

41c Bothriochloa insculpta

41d Bothriochloa insculpta

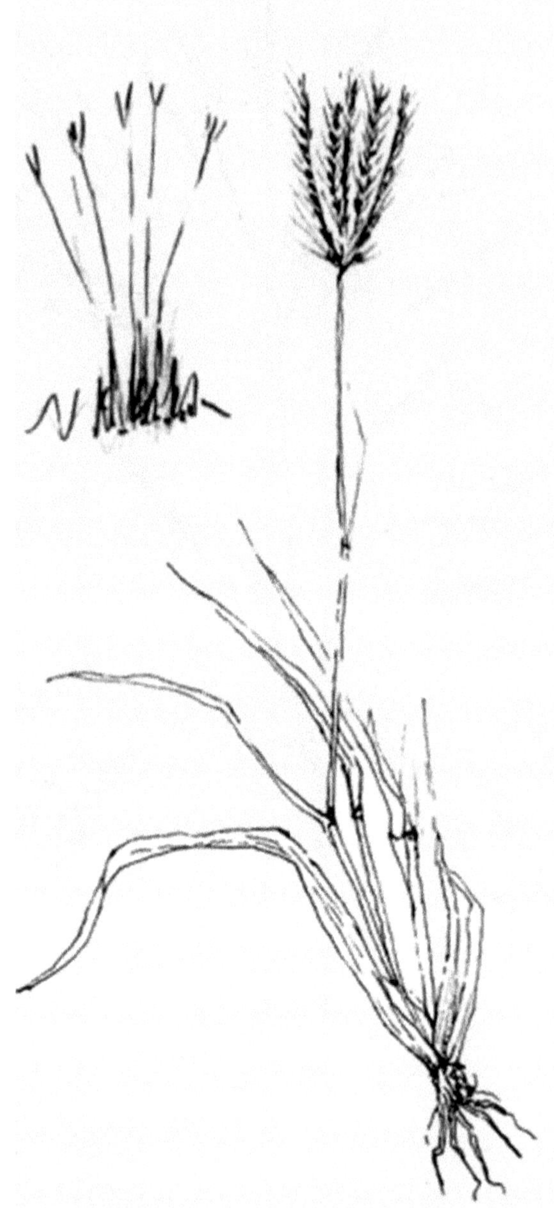

42 Chloris virgata

43 Chloris gayana

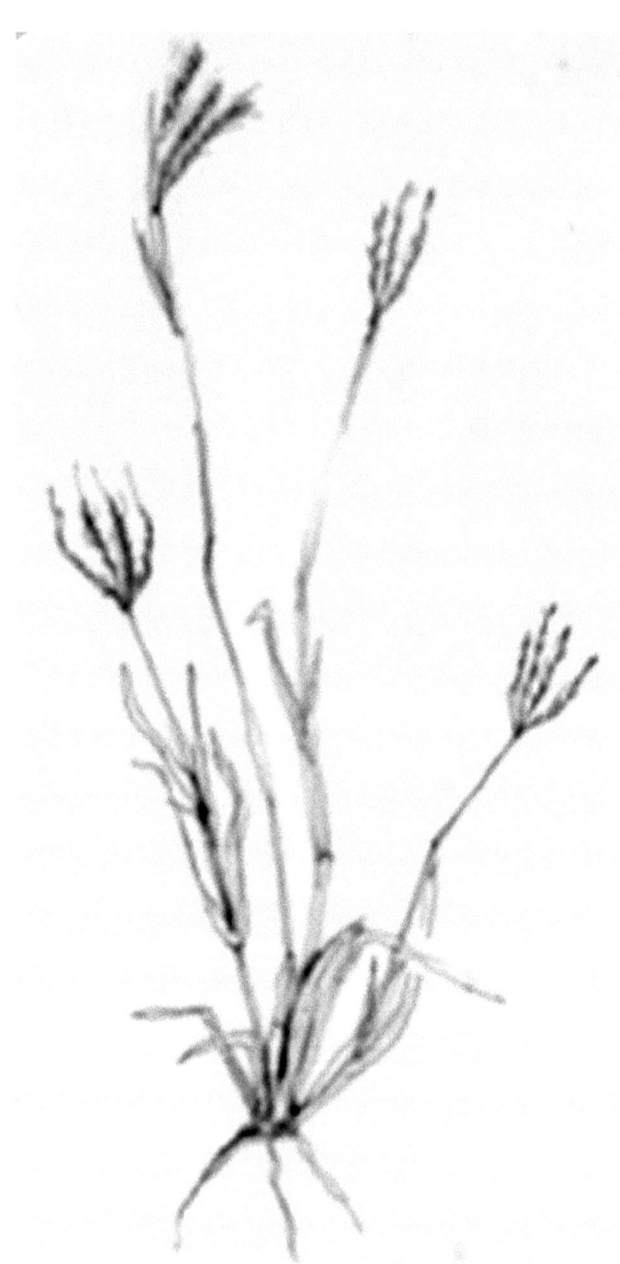

44 Cynodon dactylon

45a Dactyloctenium aegyptium

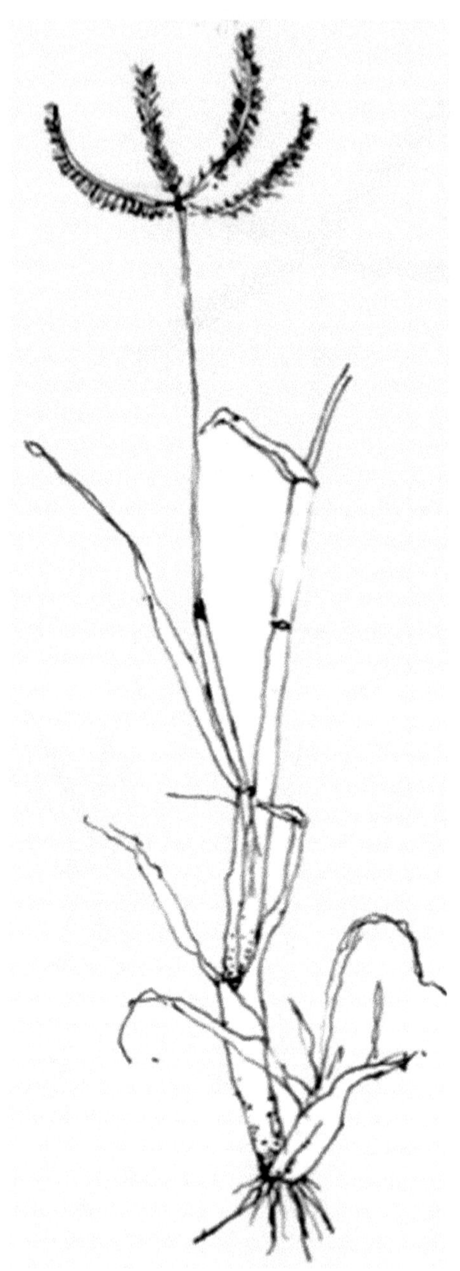

45b Dactyloctenium aegyptium

46 Dactyloctenium giganteum

47 Digitaria diagonalis

48 Digitaria milanjiana

49a Echinochloa colona

49b Echinochloa colona

50 Eleusine africana

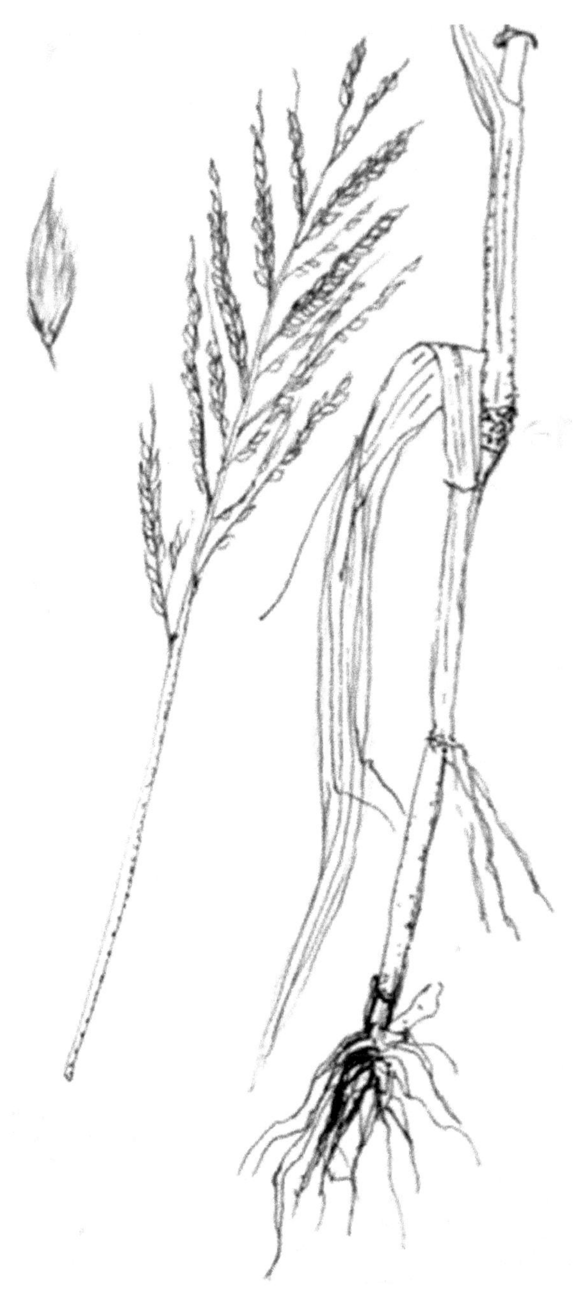

51a Eriochloa stapfiana

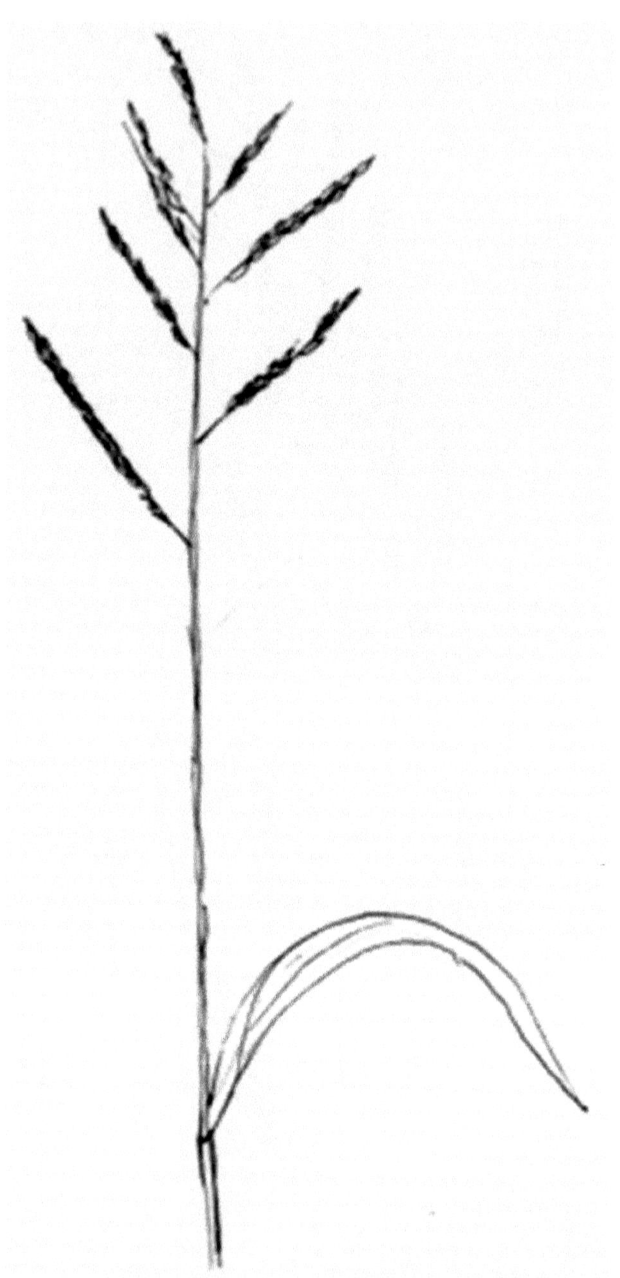

51b Eriochloa stapfiana

52a Oplismenus hirtellus

52b Oplismenus hirtellus

53 Pogonarthria squarrosa

54 Setaria homonyma

55 Trichoneura grandiglumis

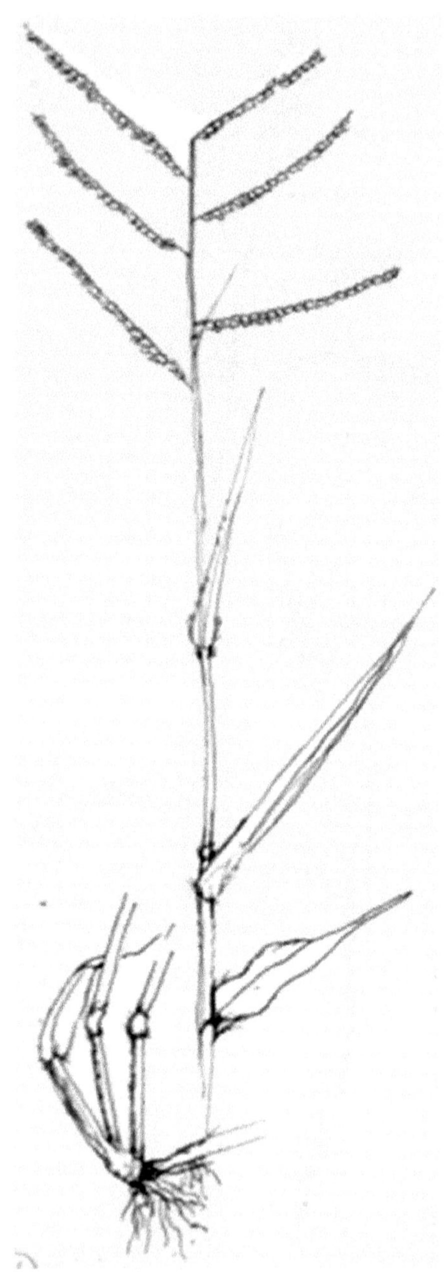

56 Urochloa mosambicensis

9 | References

Astle, W.L., Phiri, P.S.M., and Prince, S.D. 1997. Dictionary of vernacular-scientific names of plants of the mid-Luangwa valley, Zambia. Kirkia. Volume 16. 2. P. 161-203.

Lightfoot, C. 1970. Common Veld Grasses of Rhodesia (Zimbabwe). Natural Resources Board of Rhodesia (Zimbabwe).

Smith, P. P. 1997. A preliminary checklist of the vascular plants of the North Luangwa National Park, Zambia. Kirkia. Volume 16. 2. P. 215 – 217.

Oudtshoorn, F. van. 1999. Guide to Grasses of Southern Africa. Briza Publications, Pretoria, RSA.

Also referenced: https://www.zambiaflora.com

www.ingramcontent.com/pod-product-compliance
Ingram Content Group UK Ltd.
Pitfield, Milton Keynes, MK11 3LW, UK
UKHW022000190726
13853UKWH00004B/1633

9 789982 241601